THE ECONOMICS
OF THE
EURO-CURRENCY SYSTEM

PROBLEMS OF ECONOMIC INTEGRATION

General Editor: GEORGE W. McKENZIE

The Economics
of the
Euro-Currency System

GEORGE W. McKENZIE
University of Southampton

A HALSTED PRESS BOOK

JOHN WILEY & SONS
New York — Toronto

© George W. McKenzie 1976

First published in the United Kingdom 1976 by
The Macmillan Press Ltd

First published in the U.S.A. by
Halsted Press, a Division of
John Wiley & Sons, Inc.,
New York

Printed in Great Britain by
The Anchor Press Ltd
Tiptree, Essex

Library of Congress Cataloging in Publication Data

McKenzie, George W
    The economics of the Euro-Currency system.

    (Problems of economic integration)
    Bibliography; p.
    Includes index.
    1. Euro-dollar market. 2. Euro-bond market.
3. International finance. I. Title.
HG3881.M272   1976   332.4'54   75-38830
ISBN 0 470-15222-2

Contents

71401

Preface

Since the Second World War, the economies of Europe, North America, Japan and the developing world have become increasingly interdependent. This has taken place at various levels. On the one hand, we have seen the formation and growth of a formal organisation, the European Economic Community, whose aim it is to strengthen existing political and economic ties amongst its members. But interdependence is not solely the result of legal treaties; it is the outcome of economic innovation and evolution. The growth of multinational corporations, the development of the euro-currency system and the rapid expansion of international trade are but examples of the trend.

Yet closer economic ties between nations have been a mixed blessing. It is no longer possible for governments to formulate national policy objectives without carefully considering their implications for the rest of the world. Monetary, fiscal, antitrust and social measures now have widespread implications beyond national frontiers. How to cope with the complex implications of petroleum price increases is but one example of the sort of problem characteristic of an economically interdependent world.

International economic interdependence, despite its critical importance, is an issue that is frequently neglected in discussions of economic theory and policy, particularly in economics textbooks. The purpose of this series is to fill this gap by providing critical surveys and analyses of specific economic linkages between nations. In this particular volume I examine both theoretical and practical implications of the euro-currency system. It is hoped that this and the other volumes in the series will appeal not only to students, researchers and government bodies working in the field of international economics but also to those dealing with problems of industrial organisation, monetary economics and other aspects of public policy which have traditionally been studied from a more narrow, national viewpoint.

At this point, I would like to thank David Pearce of Leicester University for encouraging me to pursue my idea for this series. Macmillan and the Halsted Press Division of John Wiley have also been extremely helpful, ensuring that the series should potentially reach a wide audience. With respect to this particular volume, I would like to express my gratitude to those who read and commented upon either individual chapters or the entire manuscript: Ingo Walter of New York University, Geoffrey Wood of the City University of London, Ronald Shone of Sheffield University and David Rowan and Maurice

Townsend of Southampton University. Although I have made many amendments in the light of their criticisms, it is myself, of course, who must remain responsible for any remaining errors and ambiguities.

Southampton University   George W. McKenzie

I

Introduction

Traditionally, when someone obtained a foreign-currency asset, whether it be a bank deposit, a bond or some other financial instrument, he would acquire a claim on a bank or corporation in the country whose currency was involved. Thus a deposit held by a German citizen and denominated in dollars would be held in a U.S. bank. Similarly, bonds denominated in dollars would be those issued by a U.S. company. However, this view of the world is no longer an accurate representation of international financial transactions. It is quite possible for a European citizen to hold a deposit denominated in dollars but which would be held at a bank located in London, Zürich, Frankfurt or some other major financial centre. This deposit is called a *euro-dollar deposit*. In general, any such deposit located at a bank in one country but denominated in the currency of another is called a *euro-currency deposit*. Similarly, a bond denominated in dollars and issued, for example, by a German or French company is labelled a *euro-dollar bond*. In addition, euro-bonds may be denominated in other currencies as well. Institutions dealing in these financial instruments comprise what is commonly referred to as the *euro-currency system*.

Although several books have been written on various aspects of the euro-currency system prior to the publication of this volume, all have been written with a fairly specialised banking or academic readership in mind. None has appealed to the undergraduate or graduate student studying either international monetary economics or domestic monetary policy and institutions. Such a deficiency could be understood if this topic were covered in textbooks dealing with either of the two fields. But, unfortunately, such is not the case. Almost without exception, textbooks devote at most a few cursory pages to the euro-currency system, almost as an afterthought. Yet as the experience of the 1960s and the first half of the 1970s has revealed, the system has created an important linkage between the financial markets of the major industrial countries and provided a staging area for speculative attacks against currencies which periodically appear as 'weak' and in favour of those which are 'strong'.

There are several reasons for this apparent neglect. First, until recently, many economists have believed that international financial linkages, though theoretically interesting, were weak and unimportant. This situation became clear to me in 1969 following a pedagogic essay that I had written examining the implications of alternative exchange-rate mechanisms.[1] One central banker, in conversation, frankly admitted that, despite empirical work to the contrary, he felt that capital flows were not very responsive to international interest-rate differentials. Another central banker (from a different country than the first) firmly stated his belief that in the modern world there was no such thing as an automatic adjustment mechanism. These views were made explicit in comments by Furth[2] and Prager.[3] Yet as events have shown, capital flows between currencies via the euro-currency system have had a significant impact on exchange rates and have tended to thwart attempts by various monetary authorities to achieve domestic economic objectives.

A second reason for the neglect of the euro-currency system in economics texts is the absence of any clear-cut analytical framework within which it can be studied. Indeed, it is fair to say that the study of (a) international monetary economics and of (b) domestic monetary policy and institutions are currently treated as if they were separate fields within the discipline of economics. Yet activities carried out in the euro-currency system provide an important link between foreign-exchange and domestic financial markets. In this volume international financial and euro-currency activities will be examined against the backdrop of the theory of finance pioneered by Gurley and Shaw,[4] Tobin[5] and clearly exposited by Moore.[6]

An understanding of the system is really possible only if we are willing to view euro-banks, that is banks operating in the system, as *financial intermediaries* providing highly specialised services to non-bank borrowers and lenders, located in many countries. But in order to appreciate the *raison d'être* for such institutions, we must first understand the economic implications of *uncertainty*. Much of economic theory is based on the assumption of perfectly competitive conditions including the existence of complete certainty and full knowledge of past, present and future economic conditions. As the basis for intellectual exercises there is much to be learned from such theories focusing on the inter-relationship between a few variables. This procedure is analogous to that followed by physical scientists, but they use laboratory conditions in which they can study the interaction of two or more variables while holding the rest constant.

However, for our purposes this is not sufficient. As Paul Davidson has written in his important book *Money and the Real World*,[7]

Many of the institutions of our modern economy would have no function in a world of certainty. There would be no need for stock market speculation, for forward commodity and foreign exchange markets, for pecuniary contracts. In a certain world, there would be no reason for holding money, nor would there be any involuntary unemployment. Uncertainty plays a vital role in the determination of employment, investment, growth, pricing, and income distribution only in a world – our world – where the future is enigmatic and full of potential surprise.

Throughout this volume I shall be emphasising that the existence of uncertainty is the root cause of the international banking practices which characterise the euro-currency system.

In Chapter 2 we shall examine within a fairly conventional framework the relationship between domestic financial activity, foreign-exchange markets and the euro-currency system. Chapter 3 continues with a discussion of fundamentals by presenting a theory of international capital movements under the assumption of complete certainty. Then in Chapter 4 the implications of uncertainty for international financial intermediation will be developed. I shall examine those factors which determine not only the currency of denomination of assets and liabilities but also the country in which these instruments are created. In addition I shall argue that euro-currency deposits can legitimately fulfil many of the functions of money. This discussion is carried over into Chapter 5, where a number of modifications are suggested for the calculation of national money-stock data in order to take into account the existence of the euro-currency system.

Many economists have tried to explain the growth of the euro-currency system by drawing an analogy with the process describing the expansion of domestic bank deposits and summarised in the 'coefficient of multiple expansion'. In Chapter 6 it is shown that no less than six different processes may be identified, but that in practice only two are likely to be important. In Chapters 7 and 8, the history of the system is explained and analysed from 1958 through to 1974. It is argued that important sources of growth to the system have been (a) differences in national banking regulations and (b) deposits in the system by central banks. Chapter 9 summarises the main points of the volume and indicates the implications of the euro-currency system for economic interdependence.

As noted above, other books have been written about the euro-currency system. Since it is inevitable that many readers will wish to extend their horizons beyond this volume, the works by the following authors are particularly noteworthy: Bell,[8] Einzig,[9] Clendenning,[10] Mikesell and Furth[11] and Quinn.[12] Perhaps even more valuable though are the commentaries provided in several official publications. The March and September issues of the *Federal Reserve Bulletin* and the *Monthly Review of the Federal Reserve Bank of New York* provide almost identical reviews of foreign-exchange and euro-currency activities. Also significant are the chapters in the *Annual Reports* of the Bank for International Settlements dealing with the euro-markets. It should be pointed out that the Bank made the pioneering efforts to establish the over-all magnitude of the system in these discussions. Periodic articles in the *Quarterly Bulletin of the Bank of England* are also useful. Other important sources of material on the euro-currency system include the monthly publication, *Euro-money* and the daily press, especially the financial pages of the Monday editions of the *International Herald Tribune*. Finally, the *Quarterly Review of the Banca Nazionale del Lavoro* periodically has illuminating articles on various aspects of euro-currency activity.

FURTHER READING

Banca Nazionale del Lavoro Quarterly Review (various issues).

Bank for International Settlements, *Annual Reports* (various issues).

Bank of England, *Quarterly Bulletin* (various issues).

G. Bell, *The Eurodollar Market and the International Financial System* (London: Macmillan, 1973).

Board of Governors of the Federal Reserve System, *Bulletin* (various issues, especially March and September).

E. W. Clendenning, *The Euro-Dollar Market* (Oxford University Press, 1970).

P. Davidson, *Money and the Real World* (London: Macmillan, 1972).

P. Einzig, *The Eurobond Market* (London: Macmillan, 1969).

P. Einzig, *The Eurodollar System* (London: Macmillan, 1973).

Euromoney (various issues).

Federal Reserve Bank of New York Monthly Review (various issues, especially March and September).

J. H. Furth, 'International Monetary Reform and the "Crawling Peg" – Comment', *Review of the Federal Reserve Bank of St Louis* (July 1969).

J. G. Gurley and E. S. Shaw, *Money in a Theory of Finance* (Washington, D.C.: The Brookings Institution, 1960).

International Herald Tribune (Monday editions).

International Monetary Fund, *Annual Reports* (Washington, D.C., various issues).

G. McKenzie, 'International Monetary Reform and the "Crawling Peg" ', *Review of the Federal Reserve Bank of St Louis* (Feb 1969); reprinted in *Monetary Economics*, ed. J. Prager (New York: Random House, 1971).

G. McKenzie, 'Reply', *Review of the Federal Reserve Bank of St Louis* (July 1969).

R. F. Mikesell and J. H. Furth, *Foreign Dollar Balances and the International Role of the Dollar* (New York: National Bureau of Economic Research, 1974).

B. J. Moore, *An Introduction to the Theory of Finance* (New York: The Free Press, 1968).

J. Prager, *Monetary Economics* (New York: Random House, 1971).

B. S. Quinn, *The New Euro Markets* (London: Macmillan, 1975).

J. Tobin, 'Commercial Banks as Creators of "Money" ', in *Banking and Monetary Studies*, ed. D. Carson (Homewood, Ill.: Irwin, 1963).

2

Some First Principles

The emergence and rapid development of the euro-currency system have imposed an added dimension to any discussion of international financial activity. Before the euro-currency system assumed any importance, the question of interest was: what factors determine the *currency of denomination* of the assets and liabilities that an individual, firm or financial institution wishes to hold? Today, in addition to this question, we must also ask: what factors determine the country where someone prefers to hold his assets or incur liabilities – where these assets and liabilities may be denominated in his own currency as well as those of other countries?

While many companies have borrowed funds by issuing euro-bonds, by far and away the bulk of euro-currency activity involves the creation and utilisation of bank liabilities. Hence it is upon these that this volume will concentrate. In general, a euro-currency deposit is a short-term time deposit denominated in the currency of one country but located at a financial institution in some other currency. The origin of the terminology used to describe such deposits is interestingly derived from activities undertaken by the Banque Commercial pour l'Europe du Nord, the Paris affiliate of the State Bank of the U.S.S.R. The international cable code for this bank was 'Euro-bank' and according to one story,[1] foreign-exchange traders and banks began to refer to dollar deposits obtained from that bank as 'euro-dollars'.

As can be seen from Table 2.1, although the euro-dollar continues to play the major role in the system, other currencies have been growing in importance, for example the deutsche Mark and Swiss franc. Not only are facilities available in several currencies, the system also offers a wide range of maturities, from over-night to one year or longer. The maturities of most deposits fall between one to six months. In addition, deposits may be marketable or non-marketable. In the latter case, the depositor must hold his deposit until maturity; in the former case he can sell his certificate of deposit on the open market before the maturity date. For reasons which will become clear as we proceed, the euro-currency system does not cater for the requirements of the small saver. Rather, deposit minimums may often be set as high as one million dollars.

In subsequent chapters we shall be examining in greater depth the reasons why such a system should have developed. Our more immediate objective, however, is to describe the institutional environment in which it operates and to discuss some of its implications for international

TABLE 2.1

External liability position of eight banks reporting to the Bank for International Settlements, 1967–73

End of	Dollars		Other foreign currencies						
	Total	Non-banks	Total	Non-banks	deutsche Marks	Swiss francs	Pounds	Guilders	French francs
			(In millions of U.S. dollars)						
1967	18120	4680	4330	470	1670	1400	800	100	150
1968	26870	6240	6890	1040	3010	2290	800	250	230
1969	46200	10460	10640	1320	4640	4030	810	350	210
1970	58700	11240	16590	2450	8080	5720	940	550	420
1971	70750	9980	26980	2750	14630	7760	2110	860	440
1972	96730	11810	35200	3620	19540	8810	2210	1360	1080
1973*	131380	17470	60720	5630	32020	17160	4560	2260	2130
1974	155690	23110	63990	8050	34220	18250	3560	2760	2270

* As from December 1973 the figures no longer include the euro-currency positions of the B.I.S. (previously reported under the figures for the Swiss banks) but do incorporate certain long-term positions not given for earlier periods.

Source: Bank for International Settlements, *Annual Reports* (Basle, various years).

economic activity. In particular, we shall be concerned with the effects of the euro-currency system on (a) a country's domestic banking sector and (b) its balance of payments.

FOREIGN-EXCHANGE MARKETS

The focal point for our discussion will be the foreign-exchange markets. There are two reasons for this. First, these markets are the centre of activity for the international monetary system. Second, euro-currency transactions are handled by foreign-exchange dealers and brokers. This latter fact may account for the frequent tendency on the part of many observers to refer to euro-currency 'markets', or more specifically, to the euro-dollar market.[2]

In order to appreciate the relationship of the euro-currency system with foreign-exchange markets, it is necessary to have some idea as to how these markets are organised. In practice they are not physical meeting places but a complex network of telex and telephone connections between those who buy and sell foreign exchange. In addition, there is an important time dimension to foreign-exchange activity. On the one hand, there is the spot market which involves transactions for immediate or on the spot delivery of foreign currency. However, there are also forward markets which involve transactions calling for the future delivery of foreign currency but at a price and quantity agreed upon today. As we shall see in Chapter 4, this price may be different from both (a) the current spot price and (b) the spot price holding on the day when the foreign exchange is actually delivered.

Basically, there are three categories of operators in a foreign-exchange market.

(1) *Foreign-exchange dealers*

These are banks, which as part of their services, buy and sell foreign currency on behalf of their customers, firms or individuals. In order to meet the needs of these customers, dealers maintain deposits with correspondent banks abroad. Thus when a customer wants to buy foreign currency for, say, business purposes abroad, funds from this deposit will be transferred to an account in the customer's name. Conversely, the dealer's holdings of foreign currency will increase when someone sells him foreign currency.

Each bank which operates in the foreign-exchange market will have some idea of a desired inventory of foreign exchange that it would like to maintain over time. The size of this inventory will depend on a number of factors:

(a) The probability that customers will want to make large purchases of foreign exchange at any one point of time. To maintain its goodwill the bank will need to have ready access to sufficient funds so that it does not have to turn profitable business away.

(*b*) The profits made by the bank from commissions on such transactions. If the profits are not very great, it will not be very interested in dealing in the foreign-exchange market and hence will maintain only small balances abroad.

(*c*) The return which the bank could make if it re-invested some of its foreign currency in other assets. For example, if the bank could make substantially more money by lending funds in the domestic market compared with the commission earned on its foreign-exchange dealings plus any interest earned on its inventory of foreign currency, then it will only want to maintain a minimal deposit at its foreign correspondent.

In the early stages of the development of the euro-currency system, it was mainly efforts by banks to iron out their foreign-exchange positions that accounted for the bulk of activity. A London bank that was short of dollars would arrange a short-term loan from another bank holding an excess. As Einzig has pointed out,[3] the foreign-exchange departments of banks already had the facilities and contacts to arrange for such transfers and hence it was natural that they should assume the task. Their specialist knowledge enables them to ascertain conditions abroad and to assess the credit-worthiness of potential borrowers. When deposits from and loans to non-bank customers (for example foreign traders and international corporations) assumed a significant level, it was only logical that the dealers should take on this business as well. By contrast, the credit departments of banks would have little knowledge of the intricacies of foreign-exchange operations. In addition, their involvement could entail unnecessary duplication since much euro-currency activity is linked in some way to a foreign-exchange transaction. For example, the funds used to open up a euro-currency deposit might have been purchased on the foreign-exchange market.

(2) *Brokers*

These act as intermediaries between banks. The first course of action for a bank faced with a customer wishing to purchase a large amount of foreign exchange is to try to match it against someone who desires to sell a similar amount of the same currency. Failing this the bank will attempt to contact other banks seeking to sell foreign exchange for their customers. However, such a search can be time consuming, and hence they will frequently rely on the services of a broker or middleman. Again it was a natural development that the services of brokers should be extended to the euro-currency system – this is particularly the case for euro-currency activities carried out in continental Europe.

(3) The central bank

The central bank's job under current international monetary arrangements is to (a) see that a particular exchange rate or target rate is maintained, and (b) ensure the orderly functioning of international financial markets. As noted earlier, all three sets of operators are linked by a complex communications network. Thus if a central bank, say the Bank of England, learns that the cost of pounds in terms of dollars is falling below the target rate, it can step in to buy dollars and thus support the market. In much the same way as ordinary commercial banks hold foreign exchange, so will central banks. In addition, they will also hold gold which is also acceptable and often preferred to foreign exchange. In either case, the Bank of England can sell reserves to prevent the dollar price of pounds from falling below the desired level, and vice versa. As we shall see, central banks have frequently deposited funds in the euro-currency system either with a view to (a) controlling the funds available to banks or (b) as a means for obtaining the highest return possible on their foreign-currency holdings. However, they do not operate on the loan side of the system.

THE INTERNATIONAL MONETARY SYSTEM

As a further step towards understanding the domestic and international financial implications of the euro-currency system, it is necessary to outline the institutional mechanics of the international monetary system as they have evolved over the past several years. In particular, it is necessary to give further meaning to the concept of a 'target exchange rate' which central banks seek to achieve by intervention in the foreign-exchange markets.

Bretton Woods

Since the Second World War the international economy has essentially operated under two sets of arrangements. The first, frequently called the Bretton Woods system, because it was formulated (near the end of the Second World War) in Bretton Woods, New Hampshire, aimed at avoiding the widespread instability and economic uncertainty which characterised the inter-war period. It established the International Monetary Fund which was to act as overseer of what basically has to be called a fixed-exchange-rate system. Each country agreed to state an initial par value for its currency either in terms of ounces of gold or the dollar. However, some degree of flexibility was possible. Actual exchange rates could vary within a band of plus or minus 1 per cent of the par value. The par value itself could be altered by 10 per cent of the initially stated value, but any changes outside this region would require the approval of the Fund.

The basic operation of the Bretton Woods system can be better appreciated by referring to Figure 2.1, which depicts the demand and supply of dollars on the foreign-exchange market at any moment of time with respect to the pound–dollar exchange rate. Consider first the rationale of the two sets of schedules. The higher the pound–dollar exchange rate, the greater will be the price of U.S. goods relative to U.K. goods. In *normal* circumstances, this will mean that the quantity of U.S.-produced goods will decline and hence fewer dollars will be demanded on the foreign-exchange market. This explains the negatively sloped demand schedule *DD*. Similarly, the demand for products manufactured in the United Kingdom will increase as will the quantity of

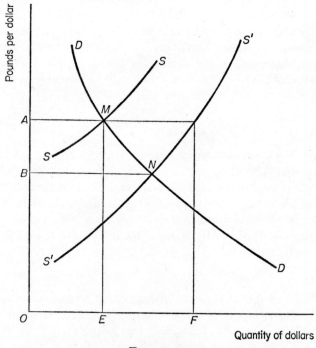

FIGURE 2.1

dollars supplied to the foreign-exchange market in order to buy the desired pounds. Hence the positively sloped supply schedule *SS*. It should be pointed out that Figure 2.1 is really only a partial description of the factors affecting exchange markets. An exchange-rate variation will induce changes in commodity prices, incomes and a whole host of other variables, and hence the supply and demand schedules will shift over time. For a fuller treatment of these relationships, the interested reader should refer to McKenzie[4] and Pearce.[5]

The initial exchange rate OA is determined by the intersection of DD and SS at point M: OE dollars are bought and sold. Now suppose that for some reason there is an increase in the quantity of dollars supplied to the foreign-exchange market at any given price. This rightward shift in the supply schedule to $S'S'$ produces an excess supply of dollars, at the initial exchange rate, equivalent to EF. The United States could devalue the exchange rate to OB thereby restoring market equilibrium at point N. If this is not done, then one of the central banks, say the Bank of England, must intervene to buy up the excess supply. For the sake of argument I shall assume that it deposits these additional funds in its account with the Federal Reserve System in the United States. However, this is only one of several possible options available to it: the Bank, for example, could, in principle, have deposited the funds with a euro-bank.

At this point a terminological digression is necessary. I shall define a *balance-of-payments surplus* as occurring when a country experiences an excess supply of foreign exchange, as the United Kingdom did in the previous example. Conversely, a *balance-of-payments deficit* arises when a country has an excess demand for foreign exchange. In order to maintain the exchange rate fixed, the Bank of England purchased the excess supply of dollars, that is its net *international-liquidity position* improved. Its foreign-currency assets increased without there being any corresponding change in its foreign liability position. Conversely the net international-liquidity position of the United States has deteriorated, since its liabilities to the Bank of England have increased without any change in its foreign-currency assets. The international-liquidity or reserve position is a *stock* variable, whereas deficits or surpluses are *flows*. As defined here, the deficit or surplus position of a country represents the change in its reserve position.

The Smithsonian Agreement

The successful operation of a system such as that created at Bretton Woods is predicated on the assumptions that either (*a*) any excess demand for or supply of foreign exchange is temporary, or (*b*) that in the case of prolonged imbalances, the authorities will undertake some remedial action including an appropriate exchange-rate change. Unfortunately, neither was the case in practice. Prolonged payments' imbalances did occur and attempts to correct them either did not materialise or they did not work. Speculators could easily forecast when potential discretionary exchange-rate changes might occur and, with little risk, move funds to stronger currencies. In other words, there were strong incentives for individuals and firms to move funds from countries whose currencies were in 'excess supply' to those whose currencies were in 'excess demand'. In this way, if correct, they could safeguard the value of their assets and make a capital gain at the same time. In terms of Figure 2.1 there would be a shifting of the supply schedule further to the right and of the demand schedule to the left, increasing the excess supply of dollars.

For the authorities and particularly for the central banks involved, the situation can take on the aura of a nightmare. In the above example, the Bank of England adds to its stock of foreign-exchange reserve assets which the United Kingdom might otherwise have spent on real goods and services. For the United States the reverse is true: claims against its reserves are increasing. In late 1971 a turning point occurred for the Bretton Woods system. In response to the large and growing imbalances experienced by many countries, notably West Germany and Japan, both with larger surpluses, and the United States, in deficit, a complete realignment of exchange rates was made by the major industrial countries under the so-called Smithsonian Agreement. However, this was short-lived. A second devaluation of the dollar in February 1973 has been followed by a period of floating exchange rates, that is rates are allowed to move more or less in response to market forces. However, the float is 'dirty' in the sense that the authorities can and do intervene to ensure that the rate does not deviate too much from a 'target' rate. In other words, the central banks reserve the right to intervene in order to damp down any 'undesirable' fluctuations.

DOMESTIC AND INTERNATIONAL FINANCIAL IMPLICATIONS

With this as background let us now turn our attention to some of the specific financial implications of international transactions and, in particular, to ways in which euro-currency deposits may be formed. Our discussion will be largely pedagogic and is based on two thinly disguised, fictitious economies: America, whose currency is the dollar, and Europa, which uses the denero. The exchange rate is fixed at one denero per dollar, and it is assumed that there are no controls on the international flow of funds. In the example which follows, a European exporter ships 100 dollars' worth of goods to America. The trade contract is denominated in dollars which are paid into the exporter's account at an American Bank A. For simplicity, I assume that this is also the same bank where the American importer maintains a deposit. The situation is summarised in Table 2.2: there has been no change in the over-all asset or liability position of the American, but simply a change in the ownership of 100 dollars on deposit there.

Now let us consider what the European exporter might do with these funds. There are several possibilities.

Situation I. He could simply maintain his dollar account in America. This would most likely be the case if yields on dollar accounts there were higher than those available in Europa and if the exporter had no alternative, more profitable investment opportunities available.

TABLE 2.2
American Bank A

Assets	Liabilities
	Deposit of American importer − 100 dollars Deposit of European exporter + 100 dollars

Situation II. However, the European exporter may desire to repatriate his funds, in which case he will sell the 100 dollars through his bank. If there is no other individual or firm who wishes to exchange deneros for dollars, then one of the central banks, say the one in Europa, must intervene. It then redeposits the acquired dollars with the American central bank. The net outcome is shown in Table 2.3. Deposits and bank reserves have fallen in America whereas they have risen in Europa. In

TABLE 2.3

American Bank A

Assets	Liabilities
− 100 dollars reserves	− 100 dollars deposit of European exporter

European Bank B

Assets	Liabilities
+ 100 deneros reserves	+ 100 deneros deposit of European exporter

American Central Bank

Assets	Liabilities
	− 100 dollars reserves of Bank A + 100 dollars deposit of European central bank

European Central Bank

Assets	Liabilities
+ 100 deneros (= 100 dollars) deposit at American central bank	+ 100 deneros reserves of Bank B

addition, the international reserve position of the European central bank has improved since its claims against the American central bank have increased.

Situation III. Suppose that the European exporter does have some use for dollar funds in the near future, but that until the time when they are actually needed he wishes to invest his funds profitably. However, if the yield on time deposits in America is less than that obtainable on similar deposits available in Europe, he faces a dilemma requiring some careful calculations. If he transfers his funds to deneros and then back to dollars when needed, the European exporter will incur two sets of commissions which he must pay to his bank for undertaking these transactions. And these charges may offset any gains obtained from the higher interest rates in Europa.

However, the exporter may solve his problem by arranging to open up a dollar deposit at his bank in Europa, that is he obtains a euro-dollar deposit. He has dollars but can still take advantage of the higher yields in Europa. The situation is summarised in Table 2.4. European Bank B now has additional assets of 100 dollars, which for the moment we shall assume are kept on deposit at Bank A, its correspondent in America. In America, there has simply been a change in ownership of 100 dollars worth of deposit. The reduction in the exporter's deposit is offset by the increase in Bank B's account. Since the demand and supply of dollars are here equal, there is no need for the central banks to become involved. Further there has been no net change in the domestic-currency assets of banks in either country. But in a very real sense Bank B's position has improved. It now has an additional 100 dollars in assets which it could loan to, say, an importer planning to purchase goods in America. Or it could sell those dollars on the foreign-exchange market to obtain deneros which it might then loan out domestically. These possibilities will be discussed in more detail in later chapters.

TABLE 2.4

American Bank A		European Bank B	
Assets	*Liabilities*	*Assets*	*Liabilities*
	− 100 dollars deposit of European exporter + 100 dollars deposit of European Bank B	+ 100 dollars on deposit at American Bank A	+ 100 dollars deposit of European exporter

But by way of summary, two important distinctions between Situations II and III should be emphasised:

(*a*) In III as in I, there has been no change in the international liquidity positions of either country, whereas there was in Situation II.

(*b*) In III Bank B's total asset position improved as it did in Situation II. However, the assets of Bank A in America remained unchanged whereas, in the previous case, they fell. In Situation I, there was no change in the balance sheets of either country's banks.

Situation IV. In the above example, we discussed a case where the individual desiring to open up a euro-dollar deposit was already in possession of dollars. But we might also have a situation where a European, currently without dollars, is desirous of acquiring such a deposit at his bank. There are several reasons why he may want to do this, but for the sake of argument I shall simply assume that the yield on such deposits is greater than could be obtained from an ordinary denero-denominated time deposit. In this case a European arranges to sell deneros for dollars which he then redeposits in Bank B (see Table 2.5). B's denero reserves held at the European central bank decline but this is offset by an increase in dollar-denominated assets which it holds with its correspondent in America, Bank A. While the composition of its portfolio has been altered, there has been no change in B's total assets and liabilities. This is in contrast to the American banking system which now finds that both its deposits and reserves have increased.

TABLE 2.5

American Bank A

Assets	Liabilities
+ 100 dollars reserves	+ 100 dollars deposit of European Bank B

European Bank B

Assets	Liabilities
− 100 deneros reserves held at European central bank	− 100 deneros deposit
+ 100 dollars held at American Bank A	+ 100 dollars] euro-currency deposit

American Central Bank

Assets	Liabilities
	+ 100 dollars reserves of Bank A
	− 100 dollars deposit of European central bank

European Central Bank

Assets	Liabilities
− 100 dollars deposit at American central bank	− 100 deneros reserves of Bank B

Because of the increased demand for dollars on the foreign-exchange market, the authorities (I shall continue to assume it is the European central bank) are obliged to intervene in order to maintain the dollar–

denero exchange rate constant. The result is a decline in the dollar reserves of the European central bank and a corresponding reduction in claims against America's central bank.

IMPLICATIONS FOR INTERNATIONAL ADJUSTMENT

Over the years various economists have sought to emphasise that there is an 'automatic' mechanism working to keep the international economy in adjustment. This idea can be traced back to the thoughts of David Hume[6] in the eighteenth century, and forms the basis for current attempts to construct a monetary theory of the balance of payments.[7] The process involved can be illustrated by referring back to the first two situations discussed previously. In Situation II, the deficit country, America, experiences a reduction in bank deposits and reserves. *Ceteris paribus* we would expect this to induce a decline in spending in America since banks there have fewer funds to loan out. The decline in spending will mean that less is spent on imported commodities, thus improving the balance of trade. The implications for domestic economic activity are less clear cut. If prices are flexible, then any decreased spending will lead to a fall in prices which would make American goods relatively attractive abroad. This in turn would act to stimulate exports. However, in the short run, it is more likely that prices will be rigid downwards and that the adjustment process will work to reduce output and the level of employment.

Just the reverse sequence of events will happen in the surplus country, Europa. Since deposits have increased at European banks, they have additional funds to loan out which should cause spending to increase. If the European economy were already operating at a full-employment level, this increased spending would cause prices to rise. If, however, there existed excess capacity, then there would be scope for increased output and employment. In the process imports would increase and possibilities of exporting would be reduced, thereby diminishing the size of the trade surplus. By way of contrast, in Situation I there was no excess demand or supply for foreign exchange, no change in bank deposits and hence no impact on real economic activity.

In these two cases, there is a symmetry of reaction in the two countries involved. However, when we allow for the existence of euro-currency activity then certain asymmetries are introduced. Consider Situation III first. Neither country is experiencing a payments imbalance. There is simply a shift in ownership of the American bank deposit from the European exporter to the euro-bank. The European exporter obtains a dollar deposit at the euro-bank, which now has additional dollar funds which it can loan out. This means that the intermediation of the euro-bank has increased the loan-generating capacity of the international economy. The exact impact of the additional expenditure depends on whether the euro-bank extends a loan to an American or to a European and what the borrower then does with the funds acquired. This issue will be raised again in Chapter 6. However, for our purposes here, it is sufficient to point out that the euro-currency system, by itself, has increased the spending capabilities of the international economy.

Now consider Situation IV, where America is experiencing a balance-of-payments surplus and Europa a deficit. If we were to attempt an analogy with Situation II we would expect there to be an increase in spending in America and a decrease in Europa. But given the existence of the euro-currency system this will not necessarily be the case. As seen from Table 2.5, bank reserves available to American Bank A have indeed increased, but for the European Bank B they have remained unchanged. It is true that denero deposits have fallen, but these have been *replaced* by euro-dollar funds of equivalent value.

Again the exact impact of this sequence will depend upon the person to whom the euro-bank lends these dollar funds and, in turn, how they are spent. If they are lent to a European, then spending in Europa may be maintained at its previous level. Further, if the borrower should use the acquired funds to purchase goods from America, the European trade balance might even deteriorate instead of improve.

BALANCE-OF-PAYMENTS IMPLICATIONS

In the above discussion I defined a balance-of-payments 'deficit' as occurring when a country's currency was in 'excess supply', conversely, a 'surplus' arises when the currency is in 'excess demand'. Since we will want to discuss in some depth the implications of the euro-currency system for a country's balance-of-payments and international-liquidity positions, it is necessary to examine these concepts more closely.

We first note the definitions of debit and credit entries that have been adopted by the International Monetary Fund: [8]

Credit entries are made for the provision of goods and services or of financial items, whether they are sold, bartered or furnished without a *quid pro quo.*

Debit entries are made for the acquisition of goods and services or financial items, whether these items are purchased, obtained by barter or acquired without a *quid pro quo.*

In addition, we shall distinguish several categories of entries:

(*a*) The current account – exports and imports, travel expenditures, transportation services, unilateral transfers, and so on.

(*b*) The capital account – changes in the home assets or liabilities held by private foreigners, changes in the assets or liabilities held abroad by private citizens of the home country.

(c) Official settlements – transactions involving the monetary authorities.

The first important point to recognise is that, as with our bank balance sheets, every transaction involves two entries in the balance-of-payments accounts. This is because every time an item is purchased, something must be given up in return. However, the reader unfamiliar with such accounts should not confuse the asset and liability columns of the bank statements with debit and credit entries in the international-payments accounts. Assets and liabilities are 'stock' variables and exist at any point in time. For example, we might say that the stock of assets held by Bank B today are worth x deneros. On the other hand, debits and credits are 'flow' variables. They occur per unit of time.

To illustrate what is involved consider the American balance-of-payments position arising from Situation IV and shown in Table 2.6. Dollars were purchased on the foreign-exchange market and hence central-bank intervention was required to maintain the given exchange rate. In this case, the European central bank drew upon its reserve holdings at the American central bank, a fact reflected in the debit entry under the category 'official settlements'. On the other hand, a euro-bank acquired a deposit at an American bank. This appears as a credit entry since, from the American point of view, it represents the export of a financial item.

TABLE 2.6

Situation IV
American balance of payments

	Debits	Credits
(a) Current account		
(b) Capital account		Increase in bank liabilities to foreigners $100
(c) Official settlements	Decrease in central bank liabilities to foreign central bank $100	

The sum of the debit and credit entries for the category 'official settlements' measures the net central-bank intervention in dollars, and hence reflects a country's balance-of-payments position and whether it is in deficit or surplus. Looked at in another way, suppose that we draw a line just above the 'official settlements' entries. If the sum of the debit and credit entries above this line is positive there is said to be a surplus. If the sum is negative then there is a deficit.

The 'official settlements' concept of a balance-of-payments deficit or surplus is only one among several measures that can be constructed. It is impossible to encapsulate all possible, useful information about a country's international-payments position in a single indicator. Where the 'line is drawn' depends upon what a particular analyst desires to show. For example, an alternative is the 'liquidity' concept which has been reported in the United States considerably longer than the 'official settlements' and is still preferred by some. Basically the difference between the two is as follows. The 'official settlements' measures *current* changes in claims on a country's official international-reserve position. The 'liquidity' concept also attempts to include *potential* claims on these reserves. It does this by including below-the-line changes in short-term liabilities to private foreigners. The rationale is that such funds can easily be used by foreigners to purchase other currencies, in which case the central bank would be required to sell off its own foreign-exchange reserves in order to maintain the desired exchange rate. Whether indeed the 'liquidity' concept as formulated does what it is supposed to do or not has been the subject of some controversy. The interested reader can pursue the pros and cons of this measure elsewhere.[9] Our aim here is limited to pointing out how the situations discussed above affect the 'liquidity' measure.

For example, in the fourth case, the increase in America's bank liabilities to the euro-bank, a *potential* claim against America's international liquidity, is matched by an actual reduction in the European central bank's deposit at its American counterpart. Hence according to the liquidity concept, America has no payments imbalance in this case. This is in contrast to the 'official settlements' calculation which registered a surplus. It is left for the reader to check Europa's position according to this alternative indicator. This and the other situations are summarised in Table 2.7.

SUMMARY

The purpose of this chapter has been to illustrate how euro-currency activity is linked to a country's domestic and international financial positions. We showed that:

(1) Transactions undertaken via the euro-currency system have a different impact on a country's commercial-bank balance sheets and international accounts than similar transactions not involving the intermediation of euro-banks.

(2) The initial effects of euro-deposit creation differ according to whether: (*a*) the necessary funds in the currency involved (in the above examples, the dollar) are already held by the potential depositor; or (*b*) whether the funds had to be purchased on the foreign-exchange market prior to deposit.

In addition, we argued that the euro-currency system weakened the

TABLE 2.7

Summary of four examples

Case	Ordinary deposits		Euro-currency deposits	Official settlements		Liquidity measure	
	America	Europa		America	Europa	America	Europa
I	o	o	o	o	o	−	o
II	−	+	o	−	+	−	+
III	o	o	+	o	o	−	o
IV	+	−	+	+	−	o	−

potential of an 'automatic' balance-of-payments adjustment mechanism. Finally, we indicated that euro-currency transactions have different implications for a country's balance-of-payments position, depending upon whether the 'official settlements' or 'liquidity' accounting concepts are utilised.

FURTHER READING

P. Einzig, *The Eurodollar System* (London: Macmillan, 1973).

'Eurodollars – an Important Source of Funds For American Banks', *Federal Reserve Bank of Chicago Monthly Review* (June 1969).

D. Hume, 'Of The Balance of Trade', *Essays, Moral, Political and Literary*, vol. 1 (London: Longmans, Green, 1898) reprinted in *International Finance*, ed. R. N. Cooper (Harmondsworth: Penguin, 1969).

International Monetary Fund, *Balance of Payments Manual* (Washington, D.C., 1961).

H. G. Johnson, 'The Monetary Approach to Balance-of-Payments Theory', in *International Trade and Money*, ed. M. Connolly and A. Swoboda (London: Allen & Unwin, 1973).

F. Machlup, 'Euro-dollar Creation: A Mystery Story', *Banca Nazionale del Lavoro Quarterly Review* (Sep 1970), pp 219–60.

G. McKenzie, *The Monetary Theory of International Trade* (London: Macmillan, 1974).

I. F. Pearce, *International Trade*, Bk. I (London: Macmillan, 1970).

Review Committee for Balance of Payments Statistics to the Bureau of the Budget, *The Balance of Payments Statistics of the United States* (Washington, D.C.: U.S. Government Printing Office, 1965).

3

A Theory of International Capital Flows

In the previous chapter our aim was to gain an appreciation of some of the basic linkages between the euro-currency system and domestic and international financial activities. In the process we touched upon its relationship with foreign-exchange markets, the money supply, international reserves and balance-of-payments positions of those countries involved with the system. However, we did not really discuss in any detail the basic reasons why such a complex international financial structure should have developed in the first place. To rectify this situation we must now return to the two questions which were raised earlier:

(1) What factors determine the currency of denomination of assets or liabilities held by individuals, businesses and financial institutions?

(2) What factors determine the country where these assets or liabilities are created?

The reason for making this distinction should be emphasised. A necessary condition for euro-currency transactions to take place is that individuals, firms and banks desire to hold assets or incur liabilities denominated in a foreign currency. But this is not a sufficient condition. The particular implications of the system arise from the fact that, in the process, deposits are created which are located in a bank *outside* the country in whose currency the deposit is denominated.

Unfortunately, there exists at present no coherent, general theory capable of answering both questions simultaneously. We can, however, draw on various strands of thought from several branches of economics in order to sketch out a fairly clear picture of the various factors which provide a basis for the existence of the euro-currency system. To this end I have adopted the following approach. In this chapter we shall deal with the first question raised above by examining some of the basic causes of international capital movements in a world of *complete certainty*. As we shall see in the next chapter, this assumption eliminates any *raison d'être* for money, for financial intermediaries such as banks or, indeed, for the euro-currency system. However, in the next chapter we shall drop this obviously unrealistic condition and examine the implications of *uncertainty* for financial innovations and intermediation in general, and for the euro-currency system in particular.

There are two motivations for following this dichotomy. The first is pedagogic. One of the most difficult problems facing any student of international economics is that there are usually a wide variety of important, interrelated variables which must be examined simultaneously. As a result it is a very difficult exercise to sort out the sequence of events arising from a particular policy action or other change in circumstances. Thus there is frequently some merit in studying highly simplified models to gain some understanding of the interaction between a few relevant variables. When this is accomplished, more complex assumptions may be introduced in an attempt to construct an analytical framework which provides a more reasonable approximation to reality.* Thus in this chapter we first examine a relatively simple world possessing complete and perfect information and then we go on to examine a more complex world of uncertainty.

A second reason for adopting this dichotomy is that it enables us to roughly parallel some of the discussions currently taking place in the theory of domestic monetary economics. As Davidson,[2] Hicks,[3] Brunner and Meltzer,[4] among others, have argued, uncertainty provides the *raison d'être* for holding money. And as Silber[5] has pointed out in turn, attempts to reduce uncertainty have lead to various innovations, such as the financial intermediation provided by the euro-currency system. By contrast, the neoclassical framework, based on the assumptions of perfect competition (including complete information and perfect foresight) that form the basis of this chapter's discussion, can provide only a *first step* in our understanding of a very complex international financing system.†

INTERTEMPORAL DECISION-MAKING IN A CLOSED ECONOMY

Although international capital flows have been an important element in the world economy for decades, the theory of capital movements is still in a very rudimentary state. Over the years international economists have spent the bulk of their time and effort examining factors affecting international commodity flows in a static, timeless analytical framework. In contrast, international capital movements involve trade in claims to future production. Hence any theory attempting to explain such trade must be based on an analysis of factors involved in economic decision-making over time. We begin first, however, with a discussion of how such decisions arise within a closed economy. Then, in the

* Inevitably, however, 'simple' theories are very difficult to generalise without the addition of empirical information about parameter values. For a fuller discussion of this point, the reader is referred to Ivor Pearce's *International Trade*, especially ch. 19.[1]
† In many respects this development parallels the three 'approximations' discussed by Irving Fisher in his classic *Theory of Interest*.[6] The first two involve the concepts of *time preference* and *capital productivity*, respectively, whereas his third approximation examines the implications of uncertainty. A useful summary of Fisher's approach is contained in Conard's *Introduction to the Theory of Interest*.[7]

following section, the analysis is extended to develop a simple theory of international capital movements.

Let us suppose that the planning horizon for both businesses and households is two periods, over which both sectors have complete knowledge and foresight. Suppose also that commodity prices remain constant. The rate of interest, however, may vary and is determined jointly by the ability of industry to marshall productive resources in each period and by household preferences for intertemporal consumption. Consider Figure 3.1 where current consumption is plotted on the horizontal axis and future (next period) consumption is plotted on the vertical axis. A curve AA' indicates the intertemporal production possibilities which are technically feasible. As fewer resources are devoted to current production, these can be used to provide additional productive capacity for future output. If all resources were devoted to current consumption, OA could be produced. Conversely, if all re-

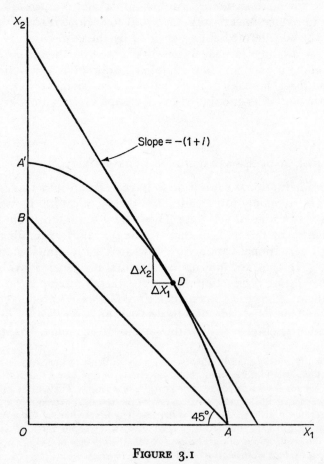

FIGURE 3.1

sources were used to provide for future output, OA' units would be manufactured instead.

The intertemporal opportunity locus AA' has been drawn so that it lies above the 45-degree line AB. This implies that by waiting the consumer can increase his total consumption over and above OA, the maximum possible initial output. A classic textbook example of this situation arises in the 'Robinson Crusoe' type of economy. Crusoe has the option of devoting all his current energy to catching fish with his hands. Or, alternatively, he can reduce his current consumption and spend part of his time weaving fishing nets from reeds and other materials. In this fashion he can increase his total catch over time.

Now let us suppose that our simple economy is initially operating at point D in Figure 3.1. If current production is reduced by $\triangle X_1$, then resources are set free enabling consumption tomorrow to be increased by $\triangle X_2$. Let $\triangle X_2 = \triangle X_1 + R$. Then if both $\triangle X_1$ and $\triangle X_2$ are reasonably small, the slope of the opportunity locus at D is *approximately* equal to

$$- \frac{\triangle X_2}{\triangle X_1} = - \frac{\triangle X_1 + R}{\triangle X_1} = - \left(1 + \frac{R}{\triangle X_1} \right) = - (1 + r),$$

where r, equal to $\dfrac{R}{\triangle X_1}$, indicates the rate of return or rate of increase in future output when current output is reduced by $\triangle X_1$. It should be noticed that as we move along the intertemporal production opportunity locus from A to A', this rate of return decreases. This reflects the assumption of diminishing returns. That is, as a unit of resources is transferred from production of current to future output, its marginal product, in terms of future output, declines. Similarly, its marginal product in terms of what it could produce for current consumption increases.

The relationship between r and the market rate of interest, i, will determine the pattern of intertemporal output. This can be seen from the following reasoning. Industry can pay the costs of its current output from its sales receipts. However, it must also cover the costs of the productive capacity used for future output, and for these no funds are currently available. The proceeds from the sale of this output will not be available until the next period.

In order to meet these costs, industry will attempt to borrow the necessary funds. If the rate of return, r, is greater than the market interest rate, i, it will be profitable for industry to increase future output at the expense of current production. This would be the case if the economy were operating to the right of D along the opportunity locus. In this region the slope of the transformation curve is steeper than the line whose slope equals $- (1 + i)$. To the left of D, r is less than i and

B

hence it will be more profitable to switch resources to current consumption. If r equals i, industry is in equilibrium. It has no incentive to change its production plans.

So far we have assumed that the rate of interest is given. In order to see how it is determined we must also consider how consumers choose their intertemporal consumption pattern. Consider Figure 3.2, where we plot a set of community indifference curves, each one representing the various combinations of present and future consumption which will yield equal satisfaction.* If the indifference curves are symmetrical around the 45-degree line then we say that consumer time preference is *neutral*. In other words, if the rate of interest was zero, as along the 45-degree line $K'K$, consumption in both periods would be equal. If, however, an indifference curve were tangent at Z'', consumers would buy more today than tomorrow, thereby revealing *positive* time preference. On the other hand if they choose Z_1, they would consume more tomorrow than today, revealing *negative* time preference.

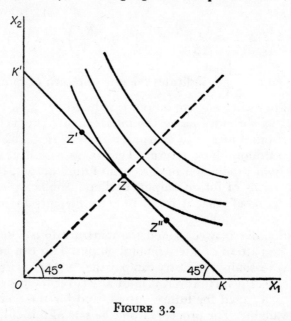

FIGURE 3.2

Full equilibrium for the closed economy is depicted in Figure 3.3 Here consumers are willing to forgo current consumption equal to AN in order to obtain OM future consumption. In the process, consumer

* For simplicity, I assume that all individuals within a country possess identical preferences and that there is a constant income distribution. This enables us to utilise the theory of individual consumer behaviour to describe the behaviour of a community.

satisfaction is increased, that is point H is clearly on a higher indifference curve than the original situation A. In order to enable this future
production, households loan resources to industry in return for claims
on their future output, in this case equal to OM. Following current
terminology, we shall refer to households as *surplus* economic units
whereas industry is comprised of *deficit* units.

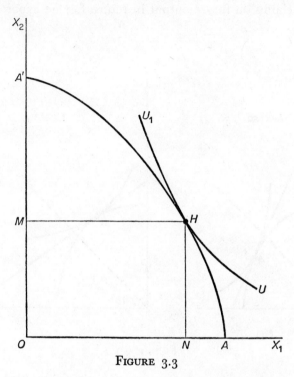

FIGURE 3.3

INTERTEMPORAL DECISION-MAKING IN AN OPEN ECONOMY

We are now in a position to utilise the above discussion to analyse the
international flow of goods and financial items. We shall assume that the
world consists of but two countries, our mythical states of America and
Europa, where each possesses identical intertemporal production possibilities but different intertemporal preferences. In addition, it should
be emphasised that we are continuing to assume a world in which there
is perfect certainty and complete information.

Specifically, let us suppose that America possesses positive time
preference and that Europa has negative time preference. Thus, in the
absence of any trade between the two countries, America will choose
the consumption pattern denoted by A in Figure 3.4(a), whereas
Europa will choose B as in Figure 3.4(b). By inspection, the reader will

be able to see that the slope of $S'S$ is steeper than that of $R'R$. Hence the American interest rate, i_A, is greater than the interest rate in Europa, i_E. Provided that there were no restrictions on such transactions, it would clearly pay for European citizens to lend in America, whereas it would be cheaper for American industry to borrow in Europa. In other words, gains from trade are possible with Europa importing claims on future output in return for the export of current production.

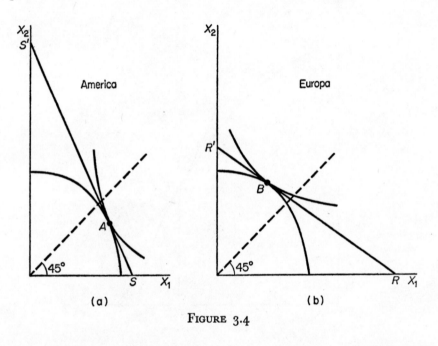

(a)   (b)

FIGURE 3.4

To determine the pattern of trade and the interest rate which will ultimately be established, we need to utilise that well-used tool of international trade theory, the offer curve. Consider the case of America and suppose that the interest rate that it faces is indicated by the slope of the line $T'T$ in Figure 3.5(a). Under these terms, American industry desires to plan on producing OD today and OC tomorrow. However, consumers wish to purchase OE today, an amount greater than OD. And tomorrow they plan to consume only OF which is less than OC, the quantity which industry desires to produce. In other words, America is willing to exchange claims on future output equivalent to CF in order to obtain DE additional current consumption.

Now this 'offer' is plotted in Figure 3.5(b). The exercise can then be repeated for every possible rate of interest with the corresponding offers of financial claims for goods being plotted. The same procedure is then repeated for Europa, generating the offer curve as in Figure 3.6. The equilibrium pattern of trade is determined by the point where the two offer curves cross at C. Here America is willing to give up claims to future output worth OA in return for OB imports for current consumption. This is exactly identical to what Europa wants to do: exchange OB units of output produced today in return for claims on future production. Both countries have gained from such trading. Returning to Figure 3.5(a), we see that America is now on a higher intertemporal

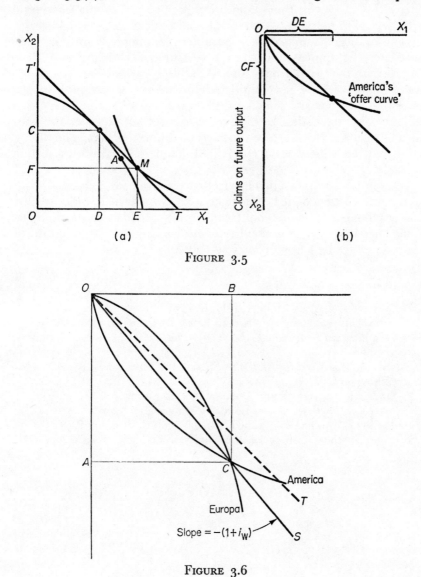

FIGURE 3.5

FIGURE 3.6

indifference curve than if there had been no trade. The same situation is also true for Europa.

SUMMARY

The purpose of this chapter has been to suggest how intertemporal preferences and production plans interact to determine the international flow of goods and financial claims and the world rate of interest i_W. However, the framework described really only provides us with part of the picture. We have not paid any attention to what may happen in future time periods. Consumer planning horizons, the life of productive equipment and the term of financial claims may all be greater than the two periods assumed in this exercise. But perhaps more importantly we have not considered the role of uncertainty and the possibility that assets issued by different economic units may possess different characteristics. In particular, we did not consider the possibility of an asset which can be used as a medium of exchange nor did we allow for the existence of specialised financial institutions such as banks.

These modifications will be introduced in the next chapter. However, what we have done here is to go some way towards understanding why economic units in one country may wish to hold assets denominated in the currency of another country. Thus we have taken a step towards understanding the euro-currency system.

FURTHER READING

Karl Brunner and Allan Meltzer, 'The Uses of Money: Money in a Theory of an Exchange Economy', *American Economic Review*, 61 (Dec 1971).
Joseph Conard, *An Introduction to the Theory of Interest* (University of California Press, 1966).
P. Davidson, *Money and the Real World* (London: Macmillan, 1972).
Irving Fisher, *The Theory of Interest* (New York: Macmillan, 1930).
J. R. Hicks, 'Recollections and Documents', *Economica*, 40 (Feb 1973).
I. F. Pearce, *International Trade* (London: Macmillan, 1970).
William Silber, 'Innovations in the Financial Sector', Working Paper No. 31, Salomon Brothers Center for the Study of Financial Institutions (Mar 1975).

4

Financial Intermediation and the Euro-Currency System

In the previous chapter we implicitly assumed that the world was perfectly competitive. Producers and consumers in both countries were treated as if they were price-takers, in the sense that no single economic unit could affect the price of commodities or securities. But more importantly we assumed that all economic units possessed complete and perfect information about all economic variables and parameters, at least over the two-period planning horizon. In essence we have described a simple barter economy involving domestic and international trade in current output and claims to future output. Producers pay their workers with that current output or claims to future output. In turn, the claims, when they come due, will be paid off with commodities as well. In such a world there is no need for money or a medium of exchange.

In this chapter we are going to examine the implications of a more realistic environment where economic units do not possess complete information or perfect foresight. Rather there exists *uncertainty* not only about what the future holds but also about the nature of the current period's economic environment. The key implication of uncertainty is that it imposes costs on the carrying out of transactions between economic units. For example, in a barter economy such as we described in the previous chapter, but one lacking complete information, any single individual or firm actually wishing to buy or sell some item may have to go through an extensive search procedure before someone can be found whose wants are reciprocal. Such a search can be costly both in terms of time and effort and in terms of actual expenses incurred in trying to communicate with potential trading partners. Further, inter-temporal planning takes on a new dimension in comparison with our previous analysis. Lacking a crystal ball, households and firms must resign themselves to the fact that any plans that they make may not be fulfilled. Mistakes may be made. Realising this, they may, of course, try to reduce the possibility of errors by undertaking studies of what other economic units may be doing. However, this again involves costs.

Except perhaps with rare exceptions, it has been human nature to attempt to reduce as much as possible the costs associated with operating in an uncertain world. This in turn has led to the development of certain financial innovations, of which three will be particularly important for understanding the nature of the euro-currency system.

(*a*) The use of 'money' to carry out transactions. As we shall see in this chapter, a strong case can be made for treating euro-currency deposits as 'money' since they are highly substitutable with ordinary chequing deposits which do function as media of exchange.

(*b*) The practice of utilising middlemen, such as brokers, to bring potential buyers and sellers together. With respect to the euro-currency system, euro-banks and brokers are in a position to fulfil many of the preferences of deficit and surplus economic units residing in different nations.

(*c*) The development of financial intermediaries capable of *transmuting* liabilities with certain properties into assets with different characteristics. As we have already intimated, euro-banks simply do not buy funds from one economic unit for resale to another, charging a commission in the process. Rather, as we shall see in this and subsequent chapters, they borrow funds for relatively short periods of time and then lend them to deficit units for longer periods. In addition, the currency of denomination of the liabilities and assets thereby created may be entirely different.

THE MEANING AND USE OF MONEY

One of the most significant financial developments in the history of man has been the practice of utilising some asset as a medium of exchange. In the past, many items have performed this function: in simpler economies, shells and beads have been used; for a long time gold and silver were used by the major economic powers. During the Second World War cigarettes were used as a medium of exchange in prisoner-of-war camps. But in modern economies the dominant media of exchange are currency, in the form of bank notes and coins, and cheques written against bank deposits. The key factor determining whether an item can function as 'money' is that it be accepted by all transactors, thereby enabling them to reduce their search costs to a minimum. In a barter economy, when someone wants food or clothing, he must find a grocer or clothier who in turn wants to buy his services. Alternatively, the potential buyer can carry with him various items which he can use to strike a bargain. But again there is no guarantee that wants can be matched.

However, in a modern, monetary economy, goods and services bought from one source can be exchanged for money which in turn can be used to purchase other goods or services from someone else. As a result there does not have to be a simultaneous, one-to-one correspondence of wants for trade to take place. Rather there is substantial leeway for patterns of income and expenditure to diverge and this leaves considerable scope for economic specialisation. A worker can undertake the occupation of his choice, be paid in money (not goods) and then spend these funds to buy whatever he likes over whatever time period he chooses. Conversely, firms will generate a more or less continuous flow of funds from the daily sales of its products but can pay salaries at fortnightly or monthly intervals, thereby cutting down on accounting costs.

Because a period of time will usually elapse between an economic unit receiving its income and making its expenditure, a medium of exchange will also act as a *store of value*: it must be capable of being held for periods of time without significantly losing its purchasing power in terms of goods and services. The question then inevitably arises as to why the primary securities issued by the business sector, as in the analysis of the previous chapter, could not in practice be used as media of exchange. Again the answer has to do with the existence of uncertainty. For one thing, between the time that a company borrows money and the time that it is due to be repaid, it could experience an unforeseen decline in sales or an increase in costs. This, in turn, might reduce the funds available to the company for repaying the loan and thus force it into bankruptcy. In this case the primary securities would be worthless.

Secondly, businesses usually borrow for longer than the short period of time assumed in our previous example. But this means that lenders will have to think of their own circumstances. If some unforeseen event should arise, the lender may wish to draw on his savings. The borrower might agree to redeem the loan but then this places a burden on him to find another lender who will provide funds on similar terms. More likely, however, will be the existence of a *secondary market* for these securities which involves the utilisation of middlemen and brokers to bring buyers and sellers together. This has two implications. First, market conditions may have changed between the time when a lender purchases securities and when he desires to sell them. Thus the possibility arises that the price realised from the sale will be less than the price originally paid in: in other words, there is potential for capital losses. Second, the security brokers will charge a commission for linking up potential buyers and sellers. Thus carrying out transactions may be relatively costly, involving a fee usually consisting of a fixed minimum component and a variable component depending upon the size of the transaction. It should be emphasised that, under these circumstances, the broker's task will not be easy, for he will have to match the desires of someone who wishes to exchange securities for commodities with someone whose wants are just the opposite. This situation is really only one step removed from a barter economy. Obviously, the use of primary securities to perform the role of money is not completely desirable.

However, let us now suppose that there exist two financial assets in our simple economy: one which pays no interest; the other which is fixed in value in terms of the first asset and yields a known rate of return. If there were no costs involved in transferring between the two, the first asset would cease to exist. Money would consist solely of the second asset, which enables both consumers and firms to earn interest during periods between receipt of funds and expenditure. However, the existence of brokers' fees, bank charges, book-keeping costs and plain old psychological inconvenience will, in practice, render the above two assets as imperfect substitutes. Rather than continuously switch in and out of the interest-bearing asset between receipt of funds and expenditure, an individual may find it more profitable to hold idle funds, forgoing any return and avoiding transactions costs.

To summarise what has been said so far, we have found that money enables transactors (a) to buy and sell goods and services more efficiently, and (b) to minimise transactions that would be associated with using primary securities as a medium of exchange. In actual practice, however, things are considerably more complicated as there are many assets possessing differing degrees of 'moneyness'. It turns out that what is or is not money is by no means unambiguous either conceptually or statistically. For example, in a modern, monetary economy, notes and coins are not the only media of exchange; cheques written against bank deposits are the means by which most transactions are undertaken. The reasons are quite clear. Such facilities are much more convenient to use than having to carry around large quantities of bulky and, perhaps, heavy notes and coins. Further, banks provide safe and reliable places for storing large amounts of funds.

However, currency and cheques are not perfect substitutes. Most banks in the United States and the United Kingdom charge fees for writing cheques against one's account although these charges may be waived if a certain minimum balance is maintained. Nevertheless there is an opportunity cost involved in holding such balances idle since they could be spent on goods and services. In addition, in both countries, some businesses may refuse to accept cheques as means of payment unless the customer is known or possesses a guarantee card issued by his bank. Even then there is usually a limit on the size of cheque that will be guaranteed.

The point is that items which are conventionally treated as 'money' are themselves not necessarily perfect substitutes. The question then arises as to whether we might also want to count as money such financial items as time and savings deposits which cannot be used *directly* as media of exchange but from which funds can usually be transferred into chequing accounts. Like the latter they clearly act as stores of value. Unlike primary securities their value, including interest, is known at any point in time. The conceptual problem involved has been clearly stated by Arthur Burns, Chairman of the Federal Reserve Board, before the

U.S. Senate Committee on Banking, Housing and Urban Affairs in February 1975.[1] He argued that

> Financial technology in our country has developed very rapidly in the past 20 years. As a rule consumers and businesses no longer hold all, or even most, of their spendable funds as currency or demand deposits. More and more corporate treasurers have learned how to get along with a minimum of demand deposits; a large part of their transactions and precautionary balances are nowadays placed in interest-bearing assets – negotiable certificates of deposit, Treasury bills, commercial paper, short-term municipal securities and other forms. Consumers, too, have learned to keep excess funds in savings deposits at commercial banks, shares in savings and loan associations, certificates of deposit, Treasury bills, and other liquid instruments, and they shift their liquid resources among these assets.

Of all these possible assets which might be called money, it is possible to distinguish two classes: (*a*) those which are means of payment by *status*, and (*b*) those which are means of payment by *function*.

(*a*) Currency and demand deposits are media of exchange because of their status: currency, because it is legally defined to be so; demand deposits, because of tradition. Both *physically* perform the function of medium of exchange; both are generally acceptable in the settlement of debt. They comprise what is frequently labelled M_1.

(*b*) However, as Burns has pointed out, other assets can function as money even though they cannot be physically used to carry out transactions but must first be converted into currency or demand deposits. The crucial consideration here is that, to count as money, an asset must be a store of value *and* easily substitutable into those assets which have the status of a means of payment.

Consider the following reasoning. As we discussed earlier, a modern non-barter, monetary economy is distinguished by the fact that the income and expenditure patterns of an economic unit, whether a small household or a large corporation, do not have to coincide. Now in certain circumstances individuals, but more likely firms, will be in a position to accurately forecast the timing of payments and receipts, and hence the length of the period over which they will be holding committed balances. If these funds are kept in the form of currency or demand deposits, a significant opportunity cost is involved: the interest forgone from investing them in suitable financial instruments. However, as Burns has pointed out in the statement above, there are a wide variety of assets which perform the role of money if we are prepared to adopt the functional approach. It is true that the purchase or sale of some instruments such as Treasury bills or commercial paper will involve transactions costs and that these must be included when calculating the true yield. Many time deposits have a fixed term which means that a penalty may be involved if they are cashed in early.

Thus they are not truly liquid. However, in many cases time deposits in the form of certificates of deposit are negotiable. In addition, in certain countries such as the United Kingdom, it is possible to place otherwise idle funds in deposit accounts with no penalties borne upon withdrawal provided that seven-days' notice is given. Even though it is not possible to write cheques against such accounts, for all intents and purposes they are *perfect substitutes* for funds in ordinary demand deposits. It is a simple matter to arrange for the transfer of funds from one account to another. Sophisticated individuals and firms may plan their asset portfolios in such a way that funds are available on or near the day that they are required.

We are now in a position to make clear the implications of this discussion for the euro-currency system. Basically, euro-currency deposits are time deposits, with the system providing the investor with a wide range of maturities in which to invest, from over-night to more than a year. In addition, certain deposits may be negotiable. Thus the finance officer of a company could arrange for euro-currency deposits to fall due on dates when it is anticipated that funds will be required to carry out transactions. On the other hand, if funds should be required because of some unforeseen event, and if a proportion of the firm's euro-currency holdings are negotiable, then these may be cashed in. To this extent then, such deposits may be viewed as substitutable with more conventional forms of money. This will be the approach adopted in this volume.

DOMESTIC FINANCIAL INTERMEDIATION

In addition to providing liabilities acceptable as 'money', banks also perform an important role as intermediaries between *deficit* and *surplus* economic units. For example, consider the case of a household with excess funds which it will want to spend, say, in a month's time. It could keep these funds either in its ordinary chequing account or in some form of savings or time deposit. In either case, however, the commercial bank may loan the funds either to another household or to a business. A direct loan of this sort would probably not be contemplated by the surplus household at all. First, it would be highly risky. Even if the borrower was the epitome of honesty, he could very well lose his job because of poor health or bad business conditions, or in the case of a firm become bankrupt. In any case, a substantial and costly credit check would be required to establish that the potential borrower was honest and reliable. In addition, the required loan might be for a longer period than the lender would like. Unless a market developed for such loans, there would be no way for the lender to cash in his investment if he needed to. For these reasons, he may insist upon a high rate of interest to compensate him for these undesirable aspects of the loan. Indeed this rate could be so high as to be prohibitive.

Banks, on the other hand, are normally in a position to *diversify* their portfolio of assets in such a manner that they do not have 'all their eggs in one basket'. In other words, the risk element is significantly reduced. Further, such institutions are in a position to provide fairly *liquid* liabilities. Because each bank will have a large number of individuals or firms which place funds with it, the probability that everyone will want to withdraw their funds is, in normal times, quite small. Further the probability that all borrowers will default at the same time is also rather small. Hence the intermediary can, in most cases, allow depositors to withdraw funds immediately or upon short notice even though it has lent the funds for a longer period of time. Finally, the placement of funds in a large number of investments means that the probability of the intermediary's entire assets being wiped out is rather low. Thus there is greater certainty as to the value of the intermediary's liabilities and the income stream that they generate than if funds had been placed entirely in one investment.

It should be emphasised that the act of financial intermediation does not imply that the intermediary's liabilities must necessarily be accepted as 'money'. Commercial banks are unique in this sense. Even funds deposited in time or savings deposits must be first transferred to a chequing account before they can actually be used. The same situation also holds for assets held at other intermediaries such as savings and loan associations (in the United States) or building societies (in the United Kingdom).

However, whether in the nature of commercial banks or other institutions, financial intermediaries can have a significant impact on real economic activity. By creating a wider variety of *secondary assets* they reduce the constraints on both deficit and surplus units and enable them to achieve a more desirable portfolio position than if the *primary* securities, issued directly by borrowers, were the only assets available. In addition, the fact that intermediaries create financial instruments which are preferable to primary assets for many borrowers and lenders means that the level of both savings and investments should be higher than otherwise. And since net additions to plant and equipment are occurring faster, productive capacity and economic growth will also be higher.

However, as might be expected, such benefits are not to be obtained without a cost being involved. In this case, we find that financial intermediaries introduce a *potential* for financial instability that might not otherwise exist. There are two aspects to this difficulty:

(1) The manner in which the intermediary transmits and amplifies

fluctuations originating in one sector of the economy to other sectors; and

(2) The source of the original disturbance.

As we have already noted, intermediaries by their very nature create assets which are of longer maturity, less marketable or liquid, and more risky than their liabilities. Thus, should a bank manager wish to, he could attempt to increase his bank's profits by extending highly speculative loans of long maturity since these yield the highest return. But this may have the following consequences. First, if a situation should arise where the bank is suffering a net withdrawal of deposits, it may find it difficult to generate sufficient resources to meet its customers' requests. Unless secondary markets exist for the assets held, it may simply be unable to liquidate its risky investments. Even where secondary markets do exist, the assets may have to be sold at a loss if buyers are not available. Second, borrowers from the bank who do not have a good credit rating could very well default on their loans. If this is widespread, the bank's assets could be considerably diminished, making it increasingly difficult for it to meet its obligations to its depositors. In many respects the problem is a matter of degree. Some financial institutions will be very conservative and will be satisfied with moderate profits. Others keen to achieve high profits will seek to become involved in more speculative ventures. This is in the very nature of the asset-transmutation process. Whether such activity gives rise to problems or not depends upon circumstances existing in the rest of the economy.

For example, consider the following. In addition to the transactions motive that we have been discussing so far we must also consider the precautionary and speculative demands for holding money. The possibility of some unforeseen event, such as unemployment or bankruptcy, provides a reason why individuals and firms should want to hold funds which can easily be drawn upon if necessary. Hence the precautionary demand. However, in many circumstances economic units may speculate that the price of some asset, such as a security, is going to rise or fall, thus causing a capital gain or loss. If it is expected that the price will fall in the future, then the course of action will be to sell the security and to increase one's holdings of money where the latter is broadly defined to include chequing as well as time and savings deposits. The converse action would be taken if there was an expectation of an increase in security prices.

Now, let us suppose that the economy has been experiencing a period of economic euphoria: expectations about future economic activity are very optimistic, and hence there is a continual and growing demand for funds on the part of industry to expand productive capacity. However, the existence of uncertainty means that errors of judgement can be made. Let us suppose that industry has over-estimated potential demand and that, as a result, output is not sold but reluctantly held as inventories. Ultimately production will be cut back leaving idle plant and equipment. However, in order to pay off the loans made to purchase the latter, receipts must be generated. If sufficient goods are not sold, many companies may be forced into bankruptcy, defaulting on their primary securities as well as on loans obtained from commercial banks and other financial intermediaries.

Recognising such possibilities, speculators will sell off their vulnerable assets and hold funds in bank deposits and other short-term assets until such time as they believe that a 'turnaround' in economic activity will occur. However, as companies default on their loans, rumours may develop that commercial banks themselves are being pushed to the brink of bankruptcy and that they may not have sufficient assets available to meet deposit withdrawals. Whether true or not these rumours may cause depositors to exchange their bank deposits for currency, in turn causing banks to liquidate their assets as far as possible, probably at a loss. In turn, their sale during a period of crisis is likely to generate widespread capital losses, ultimately driving the banks into insolvency. All the benefits attendant upon intermediation in 'normal' times will be destroyed and it may very well be a significant period of time before confidence in banking operations is restored.*

In order to minimise the possibility of an extended crisis of the above sort, most countries have established special institutions. For example, in the United States the Federal Deposit Insurance Corporation (F.D.I.C.) insures bank deposits albeit up to a certain limit. Thus, in the case of possible bankruptcy, the chances of a run on a bank are minimised since depositors know that their funds are safeguarded. In addition, in most countries, the central bank acts as a lender of last resort. Should commercial banks be short of funds, they may approach the monetary authorities for a loan usually using some of their assets as collateral. Again this minimises the possibility of insolvency particularly if any difficulties are viewed as being transient.

INTERNATIONAL FINANCIAL INTERMEDIATION

As we have learned in our discussion of domestic finance, the existence of uncertainty and lack of complete information has led to the use of some asset, called 'money', to fulfil the transactions, precautionary and speculative motives on the part of individuals and firms. When we extend our discussion to encompass more than one country, another dimension is added: each country, in general, denominates its trans-

---

* For a further discussion of the factors causing financial crises, see Minsky,[2] Davidson,[3] and Friedman and Schwartz.[4]

actions in a different unit of currency. As a result the possibilities for intermediation widen. Such operations could, of course, be undertaken through conventional domestic banking channels. For example, a deficit unit in Europa requiring dollars could borrow from an American bank which in turn had obtained dollars from a surplus European or American economic unit holding dollars. The assets and liabilities of the intermediating bank are denominated in the currency of the country in which it is located. In contrast, the intermediation provided by the euro-currency system takes the form of banks incurring liabilities denominated in a foreign currency. These funds may then be lent to deficit units requiring that currency, or, alternatively, the funds may be exchanged for some other unit of exchange should it be required by some customer.

In the previous chapter we emphasised that such international capital movements were determined by the intertemporal preferences and productive capabilities of trading nations. We are now in a position to enquire further into the nature of these intertemporal decisions particularly with respect to the implications of uncertainty. We first examine some of the specific motives for an economic unit wishing to borrow or lend a currency other than that of its home country. Then we turn to some of the specific reasons why that economic unit may find it advantageous to operate via the euro-currency system rather than ordinary banking channels.

The demand for vehicle currencies

Since residents of any particular country will be purchasing commodities from many other countries, it may be advantageous for traders to hold working balances in each of the currencies involved. If there were no brokers' fees or other fixed costs involved in exchanging one currency for another, any such transfers would occur as soon as a foreign-currency asset was received or a liability incurred. However, as Swoboda has pointed out,[5] given the fact that there are fixed costs which must be borne, it is advantageous for importers to make lump-sum purchases of foreign currencies which are then drawn upon to pay foreign suppliers as needed. For the same reason it is profitable for exporters paid in foreign currency to accumulate funds abroad for repatriation on a lump-sum basis. In this way the fixed costs and inconvenience are incurred less frequently.

Most countries undertake trade in goods, services and financial items with a wide variety of partners. The above argument, if carried to its logical end, would mean that working balances would have to be held in each such partner's currency. However, just as there are reasons why only a few assets are used as media of exchange within a domestic economy, so there are reasons why only a few currencies are used in the

international economy. According to Swoboda there are several characteristics of such *vehicle currencies*:[6]

(1) it must be widely acceptable throughout the world;

(2) the market for the currency must be broad so that one operator's
transaction will not unduly affect the exchange rate;

(3) the transactions costs associated with the vehicle currency should
be small in relation to other currencies;

(4) the currency should not be subject to wide and unpredictable
price fluctuations; and

(5) the currency should not be subject to any restrictions or exchange
controls which would reduce its acceptability.

In the past, the dollar and pound sterling have assumed the role of
vehicle currencies although now a limited number of other units,
particularly the deutsche Mark, are also fulfilling this function. The
advantages to international traders and investors are quite clear. The
psychological inconvenience of holding many currencies and dealing
with financial institutions in many countries is reduced. Transactions
costs are also lowered.

However, even though the number of currencies used for international transactions may have been reduced there are still a number
of disadvantages to maintaining working balances in banks abroad.
Finally, an important reason why such deposits may grow and flourish
are differences in national banking regulations between countries. Certain desired banking facilities which are not available in one country
may be available in another. This important motivation will absorb
much of Chapters 7 and 8. However, the key conclusion to be reached
at this stage is that, for the above-mentioned reasons, the euro-currency
system may be in a position to offer deposits which have a higher return and to loan funds at a lower cost than available through traditional banking facilities resident in the country whose currency is being
utilised.

Covering, arbitrage and speculation

In addition to the demand for vehicle currencies arising from the desire
to carry out international transactions, the existence of many different
national monetary units and, in particular, adjustable or variable rates
of exchange between them, opens up the possibility of operations carried
out for precautionary or speculative purposes.

If exchange rates were completely fixed and immutable then the only
risks involved in holding foreign-currency assets would be those associated with the assets themselves. However, exchange rates do vary and
thus there is an added element of uncertainty. Under the Bretton Woods
system there was always the possibility of a relatively large, though in-

frequent, exchange-rate adjustment. Today the fluctuations that occur in exchange rates on a daily basis are sufficiently great to add a good deal of uncertainty to the activities of foreign traders and international investors. For example, suppose that an American invests in Europa which subsequently devalues its exchange rate. Even though the denero value of the purchased assets may remain unchanged, the dollar value will have been decreased. The investor will have suffered a capital loss.

However, the foreign-exchange market provides the means by which individuals or firms can avoid these risks. We have already noted that there exists a forward exchange market where contracts are available on a thirty-, sixty- or ninety-day basis or possibly longer. The forward market is most developed for the dollar, thus providing another reason why it has assumed the role of a vehicle currency. In order to see the implications of these facilities, let us examine two types of transactions, one involving covering by traders, the other covered interest-rate arbitrage.

Covering. Usually there is a reasonable period of time between the moment when a contract is entered into for the sale or delivery of a product and the moment when that good is actually delivered and paid for. This lag may arise for a number of reasons. The buyer and seller are located some distance apart with the result that time must be taken for transportation. Or the product may not be available from existing stocks. Time must be taken to produce it.

Depending upon which currency is used to denominate a trade contract, either the importer or exporter will be subject to exchange risk during the period between the contract signing and actual delivery. For example, consider a situation involving our hypothetical countries, Europa and America. Suppose that a European importer agrees to pay an American exporter $100 (the equivalent of 100 deneros) upon delivery of a certain product. If the value of the denero should depreciate to $0·90 per denero, the European importer would have to pay approximately 111 instead of 100 deneros. He has obviously suffered a loss. On the other hand, if the rate should rise to $1·1 per denero, the importer would be able to pay less than would otherwise be the case.

If the importer wanted to avoid the possibility of loss, he could cover his position by buying dollars in the forward exchange market, for delivery on a date coinciding with the delivery of the goods. In this way he has insured himself, that is he is guaranteed the rate specified in the forward contract. The importer's asset–liability position is now as follows. He has a liability to pay $100 to the American exporter. This is exactly matched by his forward contract, an asset worth $100. If he had not covered his position, he would be maintaining a short open position.

It is short in the sense that his foreign liabilities are greater than his foreign assets. The converse would be referred to as a long open position.

The forward exchange market is not the only vehicle by which the importer can cover himself against the possibility of an undesirable exchange-rate movement. He could borrow sufficient funds in Europa, buy dollars spot and invest them in America for the requisite period of time. Whether he does this or uses the forward market depends upon which operation costs less.* For simplicity let us suppose that the $100 are due to be paid one year from now. At the end of the year the importer must pay back the amount borrowed, Z, plus interest, that is

$$Z\,(1+r_{\mathrm{E}}),$$

where r_{E} is the interest rate at which the importer borrows funds in Europa. In return he receives from his American investment $100, that is

$$Z e_{\mathrm{s}}\,(1+r_{\mathrm{A}}) = \$100, \tag{4.1}$$

where e_{s} is the dollar/denero spot exchange rate and r_{A} the interest rate obtainable in America. If we multiply equation (4.1) by $(1+r_{\mathrm{E}})$ and rearrange terms we have an expression for the cost of this covering operation which is

$$Z(1+r_{\mathrm{E}}) = \frac{\$100\,(1+r_{\mathrm{E}})}{e_{\mathrm{s}}\,(1+r_{\mathrm{A}})}. \tag{4.2}$$

If, instead, the importer had operated in the forward market he could have bought $100 for delivery one year hence for X deneros, that is

$$X e_{\mathrm{f}} = \$100,$$

where e_{f} is the dollar/denero forward rate. The cost of this operation is thus

$$\frac{\$100}{e_{\mathrm{f}}}. \tag{4.3}$$

Which operation will actually be undertaken depends on the costs of each. If $[1+r_{\mathrm{E}}]\,/\,[e_{\mathrm{s}}(1+r_{\mathrm{A}})]$ is greater than $1/e_{\mathrm{f}}$ importers will prefer to cover by a forward transaction. If the inequality is reversed, they will prefer a spot transaction. If the two expressions are equal, European importers will be indifferent between the two procedures.

Covered interest arbitrage. Now let us consider the case of a European investor who is interested in placing his funds where they will obtain the highest yield but does not want to expose himself to undesirable exchange-rate movements. If he has X deneros to invest he could buy

* And, of course, it depends on whether or not legal restrictions exist.

European securities yielding r_E. At the end of a year he would possess

$$X(1 + r_E). \tag{4.4}$$

However, he could exchange his X deneros for dollars at the current exchange rate e_s and then invest the funds in America with a yield r_A. In this case, at the end of the year he would possess dollars equal to

$$Xe_s (1 + r_A).$$

However, there is no guarantee that, over the coming year, the exchange rate will not vary so as to make this investment unprofitable when converted back into deneros. To avoid any potential losses he can sell the dollars forward with the result that at the end of the year he receives deneros equal to

$$\frac{Xe_s (1 + r_A)}{e_f}. \tag{4.5}$$

This latter operation is called covered interest-rate arbitrage. Whether it is undertaken or whether funds are invested at home will, of course, depend upon whether expression (4.5) is greater than (4.4). If it is less, then European investors will find it more profitable to invest in Europe.

Speculation. Of course, individuals may not want to cover but instead may wish to deliberately maintain an open foreign-exchange position. This is likely to occur when traders, investors and others operating in the foreign-exchange market have a very strong belief that their own currency is going to be devalued relative to others. For example, under the Bretton Woods system a situation could arise where it seemed inevitable that a country would devalue after a long series of balance-of-payments deficits. The risk of the rate appreciating would obviously be very small. Hence the possibility of incurring a capital loss on an uncovered foreign-exchange position would be remote. In this case it would be advantageous for foreigners to accumulate liabilities denominated in the weak currency and for the country's own residents to obtain assets in strong currencies.

THE EURO-CURRENCY SYSTEM

We are now, finally, in a position to discuss the role of the euro-currency system. On the basis of our previous discussion, it is easy to see that (*a*) the operations of euro-banks can be conceived of as another form of financial intermediation, and (*b*) that euro-bank liabilities can be classified as 'money' in the sense that they are functionally substitutable for assets which are physically media of exchange. There are several specific reasons why this is the case.

Economies of scale

As we noted above, financial intermediaries are in a position to take advantage of certain *economies of scale*. In the case of the euro-currency system there are several. First, the system really operates on a wholesale basis involving deposits and loans of large size. This means that any fixed costs of processing transactions can be spread out so as to enable low profit margins. Thus euro-banks are in a position to be highly competitive with alternative financial instruments on both the loan and deposit sides. Second, the fact that euro-currency transactions are carried out within the foreign-exchange departments of banks means that transactions costs can be lowered by eliminating any duplication of paper work that might occur if bank loan departments were also involved. Third, reduction in costs also arises from the development of vehicle currencies. The fact that the dollar and a few other currencies account for the bulk of euro-currency activity means that banks need hire only specialists in these currencies. Fourth, typically euro-banks specialise in their operations, dealing only with customers well-known to them and hence possessing well-established credit ratings. Thus the risk of default on loans is less than it might otherwise be. In fact, typically euro-banks do not require any collateral for their loans, a situation which, of course, is advantageous to potential borrowers.

Technical advantages

Even though the number of currencies dominating international financial transactions is relatively small there are a number of technical disadvantages to maintaining deposits outside one's own country. For one thing, there is a considerable time difference between New York and London and continental financial centres. It is, therefore, not surprising that many individuals and firms would prefer to maintain their foreign-currency holdings in their own country at a bank whose business hours are roughly parallel to their own. In addition, European residents may simply prefer to deal with banks where a personal working relationship is easily assured. If an individual or firm maintains all of its funds at one bank, the latter is in a much better position to assess the credit-worthiness of its customer. Should the time arise when that individual or firm needs to borrow funds, it will thereby be much better placed to draw on the bank's resources and to obtain a favourable borrowing rate. While possible, it is more difficult to establish a good working relationship with a bank several thousand miles away.

Differences in banking regulations

An important stimulus to the financial intermediating activities of the euro-currency system has been differences in banking regulations between the United States and Europe. These will be discussed in detail in Chapters 7 and 8, but a few words are in order at this juncture. Differences in regulations may take various forms. Certain desired banking facilities may not be allowed in one country but will be available in another. For example, in the United States interest payments are prohibited on time deposits of less than thirty-day maturity. In contrast, interest is paid even on over-night euro-currency deposits. Further, differences in reserve requirements may make it more advantageous for banks to encourage deposits denominated in foreign currencies as opposed to the home currency. A particularly important regulation, which is no longer operable, but which played an important role in the early days of the system was Regulation Q of the Federal Reserve System. This rule placed a ceiling on the interest rate payable on bank deposits in the United States. Thus at certain times when other market rates, particularly those available in Europe, rose above these ceilings, it became advantageous for surplus economic units to move their funds to euro-banks. In addition, American banks faced with a loss of deposits under such conditions found it advantageous to borrow from their foreign branches which, of course, were not subject to Regulation Q.

All of these factors enable euro-banks to compete effectively with other domestic and international money-market instruments either by offering higher deposit and lower lending rates or by providing services not available elsewhere. As a result, deficit and surplus units in different nations are in a position to achieve *preferred* portfolio positions. Not only does the euro-currency system provide possibilities for foreign traders to hold working balances in the desired vehicle currencies, it also provides an alternative instrument whereby traders may cover their open positions, as well as a means for covered interest-rate arbitrage and speculation. All of the calculations in the previous section can be redone with an appropriate euro-currency rate if it is more favourable than the rate available on comparable domestic money-market instruments. All of these foreign-exchange operations could, of course, be undertaken via domestic money-market instruments. However, the euro-currency system frequently provides transactors with more economical means.

In addition, in the past, largely because exchange rates were held fixed for prolonged periods of time, forward market facilities in many important currencies remained underdeveloped. Thus, when rates were allowed to float, many potential customers were unable to obtain the breadth of services that they desired. As a result, they turned to the euro-currency system. For example, in a world of flexible exchange rates, individuals or firms with net asset or liability positions denominated in foreign currencies and of fairly long maturity may be in a particularly vulnerable position, to the extent that they cannot obtain adequate cover in the forward market. However, a European with assets in dollars could arrange to borrow dollars from a euro-bank until that time when his assets mature. The bank, in turn, could cover its position by seeking to attract additional euro-dollar deposits or by selling dollars already held on the spot market. Conversely, a European with liabilities in dollars could purchase dollars on the spot market for deposit with a euro-bank until such time as the liability fell due. The euro-bank, in turn, could cover its position by lending the dollars out to a deficit unit either in Europe or the United States.

To the extent that these actions enable the desires of deficit and surplus units to be accommodated, it will lead to greater efficiency in the allocation of international savings and will increase the levels of investment and rates of growth in the participating countries. However, as with domestic financial intermediation there is the possibility that the euro-currency system will tend towards instability. We have already noted that banks transmute assets held by surplus economic units into liabilities held by deficit units where the latter financial instruments may have different return, risk, and maturity characteristics than the former. Euro-banks, provided that there are no legal restrictions to the contrary, may also transmute assets denominated in one currency into liabilities denominated in another. Now under a perfectly fixed and immutable exchange-rate system there would be no difficulties arising out of the intermediation process. However, under an adjustable peg or some form of floating exchange-rate system, such an open position leaves the bank vulnerable to capital losses on its foreign-currency operations. Should such losses be widespread and euro-banks have insufficient assets available to make them good, bankruptcy will no doubt ensue. Unlike domestic financial markets, there is, as we shall see, no lender of last resort propping up the euro-currency system. Should there then be a loss of confidence in the system, depositors will withdraw their funds, thus forcing the euro-banks into a further liquidation of their assets. The result is bound to be a crisis in foreign-exchange markets and a possible disruption of international trade and investment.

The above situation is not the only way in which difficulties could arise within the euro-currency system. As with most financial intermediaries, the liabilities of euro-banks are usually more liquid than their assets. Thus, if interest rates are higher in instruments denominated in other currencies, or if there is speculation that a particularly important euro-currency is going to be devalued, there will be a withdrawal of funds from the system. To meet this situation, euro-banks will have to sell off their assets, again possibly at a substantial loss. The beneficial effects of financial intermediation through the euro-currency system clearly depend upon the smooth working of all markets.

SUMMARY

In this chapter we have shown that the euro-currency system is the logical outcome of financial innovation in a world of uncertainty. An initial demand for a medium of exchange to (*a*) eliminate the search costs associated with barter, and (*b*) to bridge the time gap between expenditure and income, inevitably evolves into the use of bank deposits which offer greater convenience and safety. In a world of international transactions, an extension of this argument would imply the need to hold working balances in all currencies. But again the desire to economise leads to the development of a few vehicle currencies which are generally acceptable throughout the world. Because of convenience the maintenance of good client–customer relationships and institutional constraints, it is practical to maintain these deposits at institutions outside the country whose currency is demanded. These euro-banks find themselves in a position to transform their liabilities, denominated in one currency, into assets denominated in some other unit of exchange. This intermediation, however, exposes the system to the spectre of financial instability if for some reason the deposit base of the system should contract.

FURTHER READING

Arthur Burns, 'Statement before the U.S. Senate Committee on Banking, Housing and Urban Affairs', reprinted in the *Federal Reserve Bulletin* (Mar 1975).

P. Davidson, *Money and the Real World* (London: Macmillan, 1972).

M. Friedman and A. J. Schwartz, *A Monetary History of the United States, 1867–1960* (Princeton University Press, 1963).

Hyman Minsky, 'Financial Crisis, Financial Systems, and the Performance of the Economy', in *Private Capital Markets*, Commission on Money and Credit (Englewood Cliffs, N.J.: Prentice-Hall, 1964).

A. K. Swoboda, *The Euro-dollar Market: An Interpretation*, Essays in International Finance, no. 64 (Princeton University, Feb 1968).

A. K. Swoboda, 'Vehicle Currencies and the Foreign Exchange Market: The Case of the Dollar', in *The International Market for Foreign Exchange*, ed. Robert E. Aliber (New York: Praeger, 1969).

5

The Money Stock and Euro-Currency Deposits

In this chapter we will examine some of the conceptual and statistical problems in measuring the 'size' of the euro-currency system. Unfortunately this is by no means an easy task for we must carefully distinguish between (a) euro-currency liabilities which are held by non-banks and which may be considered as 'functional' money, and (b) those euro-currency liabilities which are held by banks and are the manifestation of international financial intermediation. If we refer back to Table 2.1 (p. 14) we find that the overwhelming proportion of euro-currency liabilities, whether in dollars or other currencies, are represented by inter-bank deposits. Only a small, though somewhat variable proportion of euro-currency deposits are held by non-banks, as shown in Table 5.1.

TABLE 5.1

Proportion of euro-currency deposits held by non-banks

	In dollars	In other currencies
1967	0·25	0·11
1968	0·23	0·15
1969	0·23	0·12
1970	0·19	0·15
1971	0·14	0·10
1972	0·12	0·10
1973	0·13	0·09
1974	0·15	0·13

SOURCE: Bank for International Settlements, *Annual Reports*. 1973 and 1974 figures are calculated on a revised basis. See Table 2.1 (p. 14) for details.

One of the main difficulties with these data, as the B.I.S. has emphasised, is that it under-estimates the stock of non-banks' liabilities. There are three reasons for this. First, trustee accounts held by non-banks at Swiss banks are for the most part excluded. Second, funds held by non-banks at institutions outside the reporting area are excluded. Third, the statistics do not include euro-currency positions for *domestic* non-bank residents. Despite these shortcomings, it is still generally agreed that euro-currency deposits held by banks account for the largest share of euro-currency deposits. Hence we shall discuss these first before turning our attention to deposits held by the non-banking sector.

INTER-BANK EURO-CURRENCY DEPOSITS

The statistics collected by the Bank for International Settlements do not distinguish between deposits held by (*a*) commercial banks and (*b*) central banks. In point of fact, the reasons why the two types of institutions participate in the system are entirely different. On the one hand, central banks are looking for liquid, interest-bearing instruments in which to hold part of their international reserves. In many respects their motivations are the same as private non-banks who wish to obtain a return on their foreign-currency working balances.

Commercial banks, on the other hand, have entirely different reasons for holding euro-currency deposits at other euro-banks. As we emphasised in the previous chapter, euro-banks act as intermediaries between non-bank deficit and surplus units, and in the process transmute liabilities into assets with different characteristics. Primary depositors want a variety of maturities ranging from over-night to several months. Ultimate borrowers may be corporations from numerous industries as well as public authorities who wish to borrow funds for longer periods of time. However, there is no reason why there should simply be one layer of banks between the primary borrowers and lenders. Depending on the portfolio preferences of each financial institution, one euro-bank might lend funds to another, and in the process transmute the liability with respect to return, maturity and riskiness. The second euro-bank could do the same thing, and so on until ultimately the funds are lent to a non-bank borrower. In other words, the transmutation process may be undertaken in a series of small steps by a number of euro-banks rather than entirely by one bank.

Secondly, inter-bank deposits may arise in much the same way they do in the Federal Funds Market in the United States. The latter is simply the name given to the arrangements whereby domestic U.S. banks with excess reserves lend these funds for short periods to banks that have deficient reserves. On the other hand, consider the case of two euro-banks, one holding more dollar assets than it wishes, the other finding that demand for dollar loans is greater than its available resources. One possibility is that the first bank could sell its excess dollars on the foreign-exchange market and use the resources to make domestic loans. The second euro-bank could perform the opposite operation, selling some of its domestic assets to buy the required dollars. However, it might be cheaper for the first bank to lend the funds directly to the second.

In another situation the bank with deficient funds might require another currency and not the dollar. However, it could still borrow the dollars and then sell them on the foreign-exchange market. In either case an alternative channel is provided for linking domestic money markets. And hence it is desirable to have statistics indicating the magnitude of such financial intermediation, not only separate from euro-bank liabilities to non-banks but also independent of such liabilities as are held by central banks. Further implications of inter-bank euro-currency transactions will be examined in the next chapter.

PRIVATE INTERNATIONAL LIQUIDITY AND THE EURO-CURRENCY SYSTEM

For the remainder of this chapter we are going to examine the implications of incorporating euro-currency deposits in the calculation of national money-stock statistics according to the functional approach. In the last chapter we went some way toward achieving this objective by arguing that such balances could be held for the transactions, precautionary and speculative motives. Indeed, in the case of the United States, U.S.-owned euro-currency deposits in general, but euro-dollar deposits in particular, may be more liquid than conventional time deposits held at a bank located in the United States. This is so because Federal Reserve regulations prohibit the payment of interest on deposits payable in less than thirty days after the date of deposit. On the other hand, interest may be paid even on over-night euro-currency deposits. Thus if we were to adopt a narrow conception of a functional money stock we would want to include in it the following assets:

(1) Currency.
(2) Demand and time deposits, which can be
    (a) denominated in the home currency, and
    (b) denominated in foreign currencies.
(3) Demand and time deposits held abroad, which can be
    (a) denominated in the home currency, and
    (b) denominated in foreign currencies.

Alternative concepts of the money stock

Before discussing further how we should calculate the functional concept of money, let us compare it with definitions currently in official use.

The domestic money stock. Fortunately, we have available an invaluable source of information about the calculation of national money-stock data in the International Monetary Fund's monthly publication, *International Financial Statistics.* In this source there is laid out, in reasonable detail, the components of each nation's money stock and a comparison with the I.M.F.'s own formulation. With only minor deviations, the official definitions used by most nations and by the I.M.F. coincide. Thus, whether we simply calculate currency and demand deposits or include time deposits as well, money is thought to consist only of *domestic* currency and *domestic* deposits, denominated in the *home* currency and held by domestic *residents.*

Now such a concept is perfectly adequate if international financial transactions are unimportant. However, where the holding of foreign balances by a nation's residents is significant, then this domestic money-stock calculation will involve an understatement of balances being held as media of exchange.

The loanable-funds concept. The major exception to the above discussion is the United States. There the Federal Reserve System includes, in addition to the domestic money stock above, all bank deposits denominated in dollars but held by foreigners whether in commercial banks or at the Federal Reserve. It incorporates not only funds held by foreign individuals and firms but also those deposits held by foreign central banks. This inclusion is justified on the grounds that such deposits provide reserves to commercial banks just as ordinary demand or time deposits. Thus deposits held by foreign *banks* were initially incorporated in U.S. money-stock data in 1960 because 'Amounts due to these institutions represent cash available for investment in much the same way as balances of other financial institutions and involve no duplication of funds held by others.'[1] Then in 1962 all other foreign deposits were incorporated on the grounds that they 'may be used for investments or other expenditure in much the same way as foreign demand balances with commercial banks'.[2] Although the Federal Reserve argues that its aim is to include in its definition of money those assets which act as media of exchange, in actual practice their concept does not meet this requirement. Indeed, there seems to be a fundamental confusion between assets demanded as money, on the one hand, and bank liabilities which provide a source of loanable funds on the other. Foreign deposits do indeed provide banks with the latter but they clearly do not act as a medium of exchange for residents of the United States!

A comparison of the three approaches

In order to compare the alternative definitions of the money stock, it is necessary to construct an international-flow-of-funds matrix. For simplicity, I assume initially that there are no inter-bank deposits and that the euro-currency system does not exist. Our analysis will be modified to account for these activities later in the chapter.

Consider Table 5.2 where X_{ij} represents the value of deposits held by residents of country j in banks located in country i. It does not matter whether or not we include time deposits; the fundamental results remain unaffected. Each of the entries in the matrix thus represents balances held for the purpose of carrying out some transaction. They are all expressed in terms of one *numéraire* currency for comparability.

It is possible to use this matrix to illustrate the calculation of each of the money-stock concepts discussed in this chapter. The domestic money stock in country i is simply the entry X_{ii}. In other words, if for some reason we wanted to calculate a 'world money stock' on this basis, only the diagonal elements in the matrix would be involved. All others

TABLE 5.2

Location of deposit: country	Ownership of deposit: country				
	1	2	3	...	K
1	X_{11}	X_{12}	X_{13}	...	K_{1k}
2	X_{21}	X_{22}	X_{23}	...	K_{2k}
3	X_{31}	X_{32}	X_{33}	...	K_{3k}
.	.	.	.	.	.
.	.	.	.	.	.
.	.	.	.	.	.
K	X_{k1}	X_{k2}	X_{k3}	...	K_{kk}

would be neglected. The *loanable-funds* concept includes all deposits located in a country irrespective of ownership. Thus the loanable-funds money stock for country i would equal $\sum_j X_{ij}$, the sum of the entries in the ith *row* of the flow-of-funds matrix.

On the other hand, the functional approach, which is advocated here, is concerned with all deposits owned by residents of a particular country irrespective of their location. Thus $\sum_i X_{ij}$ is the functional money stock for country i and involves summing all the entries in the ith *column*. Like the loanable-funds concept, the functional approach exhausts all the entries in the matrix. But as we have noted in the previous section the motivation behind the two is entirely different.

From an official point of view, the money stock is a crucial variable through which financial policies may have an important impact on aggregate economic activity. This is the case whether one believes that money matters only some of the time or that it is indeed the main policy instrument for economic stabilisation. And while there may be disagreements among Keynesians and Monetarists about the magnitudes of parameters and the length of time it takes for monetary policies to be effective, both schools view the demand-for-money function as being of crucial significance. Both are explicitly concerned with the role of money, as a medium of exchange, in supporting over-all economic activity.

But only the functional money stock effectively measures such a concept. Compare it again with the loanable-funds approach. While indeed this method of calculation should give a reasonable indication of funds available for investment, not all of the assets obtained by banks will be domestic. Part of the bank reserves will be used to purchase foreign assets; hence they represent a *leakage* from the system. They have no direct impact on *domestic* economic activity. More likely the funds support some foreign enterprise.

In many circumstances, banks *will* attempt to avoid open foreign positions, that is they will maintain their foreign asset and liability positions roughly equal. Hence one might argue that these variables should be netted out to leave those funds available for home investment. In other words, we should simply calculate the *domestic money stock*. But this also falls into the trap of looking at the money supply only on the basis of domestic-bank liabilities. Rather, attention should be focused on the asset positions of individuals and firms with a view to identifying those assets which *function* as media of exchange. Once this is done the conclusion is reached that certain assets held at foreign banks must be counted as part of the nation's money stock.

Some illustrations

Our understanding of the alternative money-stock definitions can be further enhanced by examining the changes that occur in the balance sheets of commercial and central banks in several situations. We shall continue to assume two hypothetical countries, Europa, whose currency is the denero, and America, whose currency is the dollar. The exchange rate is maintained at one denero per dollar.

Situation I. First consider a case where America imports 100 dollars worth of products from Europa, and the trade agreement is denominated in dollars. Upon receipt of these funds the European exporter immediately exchanges the dollars for deneros. Then the balance sheets of commercial banks appear as in Table 5.3. Deposits held by American residents in America have fallen whereas deposits held by European residents in Europa have increased. According to all three definitions there has been a decrease in America's money stock and a corresponding increase in Europa's money stock.

This situation is also characterised by an excess supply of dollars in the foreign-exchange market. Thus, in order to maintain the exchange rate fixed, Europa's central bank purchases these dollars and adds them to its account at the American central bank. The outcome is shown in Table 5.4.

TABLE 5.3

Bank in America			Bank in Europa	
Assets	Liabilities		Assets	Liabilities
reserves − 100 dollars	demand deposit of American importer − 100 dollars		reserves + 100 deneros	demand deposit of European exporter + 100 deneros

TABLE 5.4

America's Central Bank			Europa's Central Bank	
Assets	Liabilities		Assets	Liabilities
	bank reserves − 100 dollars deposit of Europa's central bank + 100 dollars		dollar deposit at America's central bank + 100 deneros (= 100 dollars)	bank reserves + 100 deneros

Situation II. Now let us suppose that it is possible for non-residents to hold deposits in each country. In particular, for reasons discussed earlier, the European exporter is willing to hold dollars on deposit at a bank in America. Instead of Table 5.3, we have the situation depicted in Table 5.5. There is no change in the balance sheets of banks in

TABLE 5.5

Bank in America

Assets	Liabilities
	demand deposit of American importer − 100 dollars
	demand deposit of European exporter + 100 dollars

Europa. In American banks, however, we find that the reduction in the importer's deposit is offset by the dollar deposit held by the European exporter. *Qualitatively* there is no difference between this and the previous situation. Only now the European exporter is holding balances in dollars instead of deneros. *Quantitatively* there are important differences in the alternative money-stock calculations.

There is no change in the *domestic money stock* in Europa, but it has fallen in America. No change via the loanable-funds concept occurs in either country. However, the functional approach shows an increase in money defined in this fashion in Europa and a decrease in America. Of the three alternatives only this approach gives the same result as obtained in Situation I, *qualitatively* identical to this case. Clearly, then, this provides a strong argument for including foreign deposits held by a nation's residents if we are truly interested in totalling up those assets which can *functionally* serve as media of exchange.

The conclusion is so striking that it is worthwhile to pursue the reasoning. No one ever expects export receipts and import expenditures to balance over time. Likewise there is no reason to expect that funds generated from bank liabilities held by foreigners should equal assets held by domestic residents abroad. The trap that many economists have fallen into is to treat the money stock as a bank liability and not as an asset held by individuals and firms for various motives.

Situation III. Now assume that Europa imports goods worth 100 deneros from America in addition to its export trade. Let us also suppose that American exporters desire to hold deneros. We then have the situation depicted in Table 5.6. On the basis of both the loanable-funds and

TABLE 5.6

Bank in America		Bank in Europa	
Assets	*Liabilities*	*Assets*	*Liabilities*
	demand deposit of American importer − 100 dollars		demand deposit of European importer − 100 deneros
	demand deposit of European exporter + 100 dollars		demand deposit of American exporter + 100 deneros

functional approaches there is no change in the money stock. However, domestic deposits held by residents of both countries have fallen. Thus the domestic money stock has decreased in both countries. Clearly this is an important asymmetry. There has been no net flow of funds between countries and yet the money stock is calculated as falling. The Federal Reserve Bank of St Louis has recently advocated the adoption of this approach in the United States.[3] While it would certainly put the United States on the same basis as the rest of the world, it is clear that such a measure is incomplete. In a world where there are no international transactions, there is no problem. However, it certainly fails to take into account current circumstances.

Implications of euro-currency transactions

We are now in a position to extend the concept of a functional money stock to encompass euro-currency transactions. In Table 5.2, each bank deposit was characterised by the country in which it was located and by the country of residence of the owner. The existence of euro-currency transactions potentially adds another dimension to our matrix. That is, foreign deposits are not only characterised by their location but the currency of denomination as well. Conceptually, it is difficult to visualise a three-dimensional box. However, it is not necessary if we are careful in our formulation. We must simply calculate those balances held abroad, irrespective of their currency of denomination, provided, of course, these deposits fulfil the function of media of exchange. However, since we are primarily interested in those deposits which are held by non-banks and which fulfil the functions of money, it is necessary to be careful and net out those deposits held by euro-banks and central banks. Neither of these categories *functions* as money.

The immediate problem can best be understood in the light of some specific examples.

Situation IV. Let us suppose that the European exporter desires to hold dollars. However, now we assume that he maintains a dollar deposit, not in America, but in a bank in Europa. The latter bank then redeposits the funds in an American Bank. The outcome is depicted in Table 5.7.

TABLE 5.7

Bank in America		Bank in Europa	
Assets	*Liabilities*	*Assets*	*Liabilities*
	deposit of American Importer − 100 dollars	dollar deposit at American bank + 100 dollars	dollar deposit of European exporter + 100 dollars
	deposit of Europa bank + 100 dollars		

From a functional viewpoint we would calculate that there had been an increase in Europa's money stock, because of the euro-dollar deposit, and a decrease in America's money stock. Again this is the same result as obtained in Situations I and II. We would not count the dollar deposit of the Europa bank because it was not being held as a medium of exchange by the non-bank public.

C

Situation V. Let us now suppose that the European bank no longer wishes to hold dollar assets but instead sells them on the foreign-exchange market for deneros. As in Situation I the European central bank intervenes to buy the excess supply of dollars now on the market and adds them to its account at America's central bank. The resulting changes are shown in Table 5.8. On the basis of the functional and

TABLE 5.8

Bank in America		Bank in Europa	
Assets	*Liabilities*	*Assets*	*Liabilities*
reserves − 100 dollars	dollar deposit of Europa Bank − 100 dollars	dollar deposits at American bank − 100 dollars	
		denero reserves + 100 deneros	

America's Central Bank		European Central Bank	
Assets	*Liabilities*	*Assets*	*Liabilities*
	bank reserves − 100 dollars	dollar deposit America's central bank + 100 deneros (= 100 dollars)	bank reserves + 100 deneros
	deposit of European central bank + 100 dollars		

domestic money-stock concepts there are no changes from the previous situation. But the loanable-funds money stock falls in America although it remains unchanged in Europa. This particular example highlights the implications of the double counting implicit in the U.S. approach. Even though there has been no change in deposits held by the non-bank public, the shift in reserves from an American commercial bank to the European central bank would appear to indicate a change in America's money stock, whereas, in fact, none has occurred.

The Monetary Base

As noted earlier, the money stock plays a significant role in both economic theory and practical policy discussions. An increase in the money stock, for whatever reason, is generally interpreted as representing an increase in spendable funds that in turn produces an increase in national output and economic activity. This relationship may, of course, vary. If times are bad and people are particularly pessimistic, they prefer to hold a high proportion of their funds idle rather than spend them.

Conversely, if economic activity is very strong and everyone is optimistic, then any increase in the money stock may lead very quickly to further increases in spending and, if the economy is operating at or near full employment, to inflation.

Despite its central place in discussions of macroeconomic activity, the money stock is not directly under the control of central banks. What is generally under their control, however, is their own balance-sheet position. This suggests that we should look there for an indicator of central-bank activity. For example, suppose that a central bank buys securities on the open market. There is an immediate increase in its assets. Further, the seller of the securities now has additional funds in his bank account, that is the money stock has increased. There will, of course, be a further expansion in bank deposits depending on the proportion of assets that commercial banks hold as reserves and the amount of currency people prefer to hold. As we shall argue in the next chapter these amounts may be variable over time; it is in this sense that the authorities do not directly control the money stock, although, as our illustration here indicates, they certainly influence it.

In addition, central banks, as we have seen, also hold foreign-currency deposits and gold, and changes in these variables, arising from intervention in foreign-exchange markets, also influence the money stock. For example, let us return to our discussion of Situation I earlier in this chapter. In order to maintain a fixed exchange rate, the European monetary authorities purchased on the foreign-exchange market the excess supply of dollars resulting from a trade surplus. This in turn led to an increase in commercial-bank deposits, the same outcome as produced by the central-bank open-market purchases.

However, when examining the implications for changes in a country's balance-of-payments position on the central bank's balance sheet and ultimately upon that country's money stock, we must also look at the bank's liability position. For example, in the previous case, the excess supply of dollars could have been met by the American central bank drawing down its deposit at the European central bank and then using these funds to intervene in the foreign-exchange market. However, in this case there has been a reduction in the European central bank's liabilities to its American counterpart instead of an increase in European central-bank foreign-currency assets. But both have the same impact on commercial-bank deposits.

The sum of securities held by the central bank and its net international-liquidity position (foreign-currency assets plus gold minus foreign-currency liabilities) is frequently called the 'monetary base' and is treated as a crucial variable reflecting central-bank policies. Increases in the base, which *is* under the direct control of the monetary authorities, should, it is believed, lead to an increase in the money stock. For additional discussion of these points, the reader is referred to Alchian and Allen.[4] Now it is true that in a world where it is not possible to hold foreign deposits, there is an obvious relationship between the monetary base and the money stock, a relationship that has been exploited by many economists, particularly Johnson,[5] to develop a monetarist theory of balance-of-payments adjustment. For example, a trade surplus leads to an increase in the monetary base which, in turn, causes the money supply to increase. Incomes and/or prices increase causing imports to rise and exports to fall until the surplus is eliminated. It is envisaged that a similar process will also be at work in other countries as well.

In a world such as exists at the moment where it is possible for residents of one country to hold funds abroad, the situation is different. No matter which concept of the money stock is used, there will not necessarily be a relationship with the monetary base. At this stage the reader is invited to calculate the changes in the base that occur for Europa and America with respect to Situations II through V. The results are shown in Table 5.9, together with a summary of money-stock changes according to the three alternative calculations. Not only does the table reveal the wide disparity of results discussed earlier, it also shows that there is no one-to-one correspondence between the

TABLE 5.9

Summary of examples

Situation	Country	D.M.S.	L.F.	F.A.	M.B.
I	America	−	−	−	−
	Europa	+	+	+	+
II	America	−	o	−	o
	Europa	o	o	+	o
III	America	−	o	o	o
	Europa	−	o	o	o
IV	America	−	o	−	o
	Europa	+	+	+	o
V	America	o	−	o	−
	Europa	o	o	o	+

D.M.S. = domestic money stock
L.F.   = loanable-funds concept
F.A.   = functional approach
M.B.   = monetary base

Estimated private international liquidity and official reserve holdings, 1964–73

(In billions of U.S. dollars)

Year	Estimated private liquidity holdings			Other estimated euro-currency liabilities‡			Estimated private international liquidity§
	U.S. external dollar liabilities* (1)	U.K. external sterling liabilities** (2)	Estimated euro-dollar liabilities† (3)	deutsche Mark (4)	Swiss franc (5)	Other (6)	(7)
1964	11·1	4·7	6·8	0·5	0·6	0·7	24·4
1965	11·5	4·9	6·8	0·6	0·7	0·8	27·3
1966	14·2	4·7	11·4	0·7	0·9	1·0	32·9
1967	15·8	3·8	14·2	1·2	1·0	0·9	36·9
1968	19·4	3·5	21·5	2·2	1·7	1·2	49·5
1969	28·2	3·4	33·6	2·8	2·5	1·1	71·6
1970	21·8	4·0	37·8	5·2	3·8	1·8	74·4
1971	15·1	6·2	40·3	7·9	4·6	2·6	76·7
1972	19·8	6·1	50·6	10·5	5·3	3·9	96·1
1973	23·8	5·3	67·0	15·2	9·0	5·8	126·1

* Taken from *I.F.S.*, U.S. country pages, line 4b. It includes short-term liabilities to non-residents other than central banks, governments and international agencies.

** Taken from *I.F.S.*, U.K. country pages, line 4c. It includes assets not held for central monetary purposes, or by international agencies, and excludes U.K. government bonds.

† This series is based on euro-dollar liabilities to non-residents, as reported by the B.I.S., but adjusted for identified official euro-dollar holdings (and the 'unidentified residual item' since 1971), and inter-bank deposits as estimated by the B.I.S.

‡ These series are based on liabilities presented in the B.I.S. *Annual Reports*, adjusted for identified official euro-currency holdings, and inter-bank deposits, as estimated by the B.I.S. The same adjustment factor was used for inter-bank deposits for each of the three components for any given year, although the adjustment factor varied from year to year.

§ This column is the sum of columns 1–6. To the extent that euro-banks hold dollars with U.S. banks, and these deposits are already counted in the U.S. liabilities column, this figure includes some double counting. To the extent that external liabilities of countries other than the United States and the United Kingdom are not covered, and the euro-currency liabilities exclude liabilities in foreign currencies to residents, this figure will under-estimate private international-liquidity holdings.

SOURCE: International Monetary Fund, *Annual Report, 1974* (Washington, D.C.) p. 44.

monetary base and *any* of the three definitions. Only if a nation's residents are prohibited from holding foreign balances will the measure coincide, leaving an identifiable relationship to the base.

SUMMARY AND CONCLUSIONS

The question must inevitably be raised: just how significant are the above conceptual arguments likely to be in practice? It is difficult to answer this question conclusively given the current gaps in the collection of international monetary data. What is required is that each nation's central bank acquire and report commercial-bank deposits on the basis of:

(1) The country of the depositor;
(2) Whether the depositor is another bank or is a non-bank; and
(3) The currency of denomination of the deposit.

Not only would this break-down allow a better understanding of the international flow of funds; given the important role of the dollar and other currencies as vehicle currencies, it is quite likely that such amendments will be quite important for the calculation of money-stock data.

A rough idea of the magnitudes involved can be gleaned from some data prepared by the I.M.F. and shown in Table 5.10. Here are shown the external liabilities of the United States and the United Kingdom in addition to euro-currency liabilities. As seen from the footnotes, attempts have been made to avoid double counting. When these entries are summed up, the total shown in column 7 represents an estimate of private international liquidity. Referring back to our flow-of-funds matrix (Table 5.2, p. 61) this figure provides a very rough approximation to all the off-diagonal elements. It is an approximation in the sense that only major currencies have been included.

In order to get an idea of the magnitudes involved, it is useful to compare the figure for private international liquidity with domestic money-stock data (including time and savings deposits) for several nations. From Table 5.11, it is seen that in 1973 private international

TABLE 5.11

Domestic money-stock data, 1973 *(in billions of U.S. dollars)*	
United States	635·4
United Kingdom	76·9
West Germany	190·1
France	76·4
Italy	137·4
Switzerland	42·8

SOURCE: International financial statistics.

liquidity, consisting mainly of euro-currency liabilities, was about 50 per cent larger than the U.K. money stock, about two-thirds the size of West Germany's measure and almost equal to Italy's figure. By any comparison it is quite large.

FURTHER READING

A. A. Alchian and W. Allen, *University Economics* (Belmont, California: Wadsworth, 1968).

A. E. Burger and Anatol Balbach, 'Measure of the Domestic Money Stock', *Review of the Federal Reserve Bank of St Louis* (May 1972).

Federal Reserve System, 'A New Measure of the Money Stock', *Federal Reserve Bulletin* (Oct 1963).

Federal Reserve System, 'Revision of Money Supply Series', *Federal Reserve Bulletin* (Aug 1962).

H. G. Johnson, 'The Monetary Approach to Balance of Payments Theory', in *International Trade and Money*, ed. M. Connolly and A. Swoboda (London: Allen & Unwin, 1973).

6
Euro-Currency Multipliers

In Chapter 2 we examined only the initial or first-round implications of euro-currency deposit creation. However, once a bank has obtained additional reserves, whether denominated in domestic or foreign currency, it may want to loan all or part of these funds in order to obtain a profitable return. And this means that another sequence of events will be set in motion with the ultimate impact on the euro-currency system depending upon:

(a) whether the funds are lent to another bank or to a non-bank;

(b) whether the lending bank or the borrower exchanges the funds for another currency; and

(c) the ultimate purpose which the borrowed funds are used for.

As we shall see, a number of prominent economists have attempted to explain the expansion of euro-currency deposits in a fashion that is analogous to the traditional textbook explanation of the multiple expansion of bank deposits. Unfortunately, much of this discussion is misleading, drawing attention away from some of the important characteristics of the euro-currency system. In order to appreciate the nature of the factors influencing its growth, we begin in the next section with a restatement of the multiple expansion process and then contrast it with Tobin's 'new' view of bank behaviour.[1] Against this background, I then interpret and compare the views of Swoboda,[2] Friedman,[3] Mayer,[4] Clendenning[5] and Hewson and Sakakibara,[6] all with regard to the euro-currency system.

THE MULTIPLE EXPANSION PROCESS

The traditional view of how money is 'created' depends very crucially on the existence of a fixed reserve ratio or reserve requirement which can only be changed at the discretion of the authorities. Let us take as an example the situation arising in Situation II of Chapter 2. There our fictitious country Europa had exported 100 deneros worth of goods and this ultimately led to an increase in European bank reserves and deposits also of 100 deneros. Typically, banks will not want to keep all of these funds idle and instead they will seek to make loans at a profitable interest rate. But let us suppose that the European authorities have imposed a statutory reserve requirement on the banks, equal, say, to

20 per cent. This means that only 80 deneros can be lent out, with 20 deneros held as reserves with the European central bank.

The individual or firm borrowing the funds will, of course, not hold them idle, since the rate of interest to be paid on the loan represents a significant opportunity cost. Obviously the loan was undertaken with a view to making some purchase. When this is accomplished, the business selling the goods or services will have an additional 80 deneros, 90 per cent of which we shall assume he deposits in his bank. The remaining 10 per cent, or 8 deneros, represents a 'leakage' from the banking system and may arise for a number of reasons:

(a) part of the receipts may be held in the form of currency rather than bank deposits;

(b) part may be used to pay taxes to the government which may not redeposit part or all of these funds with commercial banks; and

(c) some may be used to purchase foreign currency in order to import commodities or financial items from abroad.

If the ratios of funds lent out and then redeposited are constant across the economy, a similar expansion of bank deposits will be set in motion: 57·6 deneros, representing 80 per cent of the 72-denero deposit will be lent out with the remaining 14·4 deneros held as reserves. Subsequently the borrower will purchase goods or services worth 57·6 deneros, 90 per cent of which will be deposited in a bank. This will then set in motion a further round of expansion with the process continuing *ad infinitum*. The results are summarised in Table 6.1 through four rounds.

TABLE 6.1
Expansion of bank deposits
(*in deneros*)

Stage of expansion	Deposits (1)	Required reserves (2)	Loans (3)	Leakage (4)
initial	+100	+20	+80	0
2	+ 72	+14·4	+57·6	+8
3	+ 51·8	+10·4	+41·4	+5·8
4	+ 37·3	+ 7·5	+29·8	+4·1
.	.	.	.	.
.	.	.	.	.
.	.	.	.	.
Total	+357·1	+71·4	+285·7	+28·6

Reserve requirement = 0·20.
Currency ratio = 0·10.

The total amount of deposits, loans, required reserves and 'leakages' can easily be calculated by noting that the expansion process takes the form of a geometric series. Let D represent the initial bank deposit, which in our example was made by the European exporter, r the reserve requirement and e the proportional 'leakage'. Then during each round the proportion $g(=1-r)$ of each deposit will be lent out, and of this $h(=1-e)$ will be redeposited in the banking system. Thus total deposits, T.D., can be written as

$$\text{T.D.} = D[1 + gh + (gh)^2 + (gh)^3 + \ldots + (gh)^n], \qquad (6.1)$$

where n is tending towards infinity. Now multiply the series on the right-hand side of equation (6.1) by $1 - gh$ to obtain

$$[1 + gh + (gh)^2 + (gh)^3 + \ldots + (gh)^n] \ (1 - gh) =$$
$$[1 + gh + (gh)^2 + (gh)^3 + \ldots + (gh)^n$$
$$- gh - (gh)^2 - (gh)^3 - (gh)^n - (gh)^{n+1}]$$
$$= [1 - (gh)^{n+1}]. \qquad (6.2)$$

Since g and h are always fractions $(gh)^{n+1}$ tends to zero as n tends towards infinity. Hence $(gh)^{n+1}$ can be neglected with the result that

$$[1 + (gh) + (gh)^2 + (gh)^3 + \ldots + (gh)^n] = \frac{1}{1 - gh}. \qquad (6.3)$$

That is,

$$\text{T.D.} = D\left(\frac{1}{1 - gh}\right), \qquad (6.4)$$

where $1/1 - gh$ is frequently referred to as the coefficient of multiple expansion. It can easily be seen from Table 6.1 that the growth in bank loans and required reserves can be described in a similar fashion. This is left for the reader to work out.

Although the above analysis is fundamentally the same as that appearing in most economics textbooks, it is unfortunately not a particularly realistic or illuminating description of bank behaviour. The key, as Tobin[7] has emphasised, is to look at any growth in bank liabilities as the outcome of portfolio decisions on the part of depositors on the one hand, and the banks themselves on the other. In particular, it is necessary to appreciate the role of a bank as a financial intermediary. Once this is done it is no longer possible to consider a multiple expansion process in terms of a fixed, immutable multiplier.

Let us first consider the factors which may affect the leakage co-efficient e. In normal circumstances the ratio of currency to bank deposits will probably remain constant. However, in extreme circumstances when there is widespread fear of commercial-bank failure, depositors may attempt to increase their currency holdings. As a result the coefficient of multiple expansion will be reduced. Or the authorities might increase taxes, depositing the proceeds not with a commercial bank but with the central bank instead. This also would increase the extent of any leakages and reduce the amount of funds redeposited in the banking system. A similar situation would arise if the price of goods produced at home rose relative to those produced abroad. Depending on the price responsiveness of households and firms, the value of imports may rise whereas the value of exports falls. This leads to a net increase in purchases of foreign exchange and, of course, reduces the amount of funds available for redeposit in the domestic banking system.

Of equal interest to us is the fact that banks may decide not to be fully loaned up, that is they may decide to hold excess reserves. For example, suppose that times are sufficiently bad that potential borrowers are very pessimistic. As a result the demand for funds is weak and interest rates will be relatively low. At the same time those individuals or firms applying to banks for funds may be considered to be highly risky, given uncertain business conditions: the possibility of bankruptcy or loss of job is a real possibility. Hence, faced with a relatively low return but high risk, banks may simply decide to hold some idle funds rather than lend them out. The proportion r will be larger than the required reserve ratio with the result that the coefficient of multiple expansion may be smaller than would otherwise be the case.

Conversely, if times are very good, banks may not be able to obtain sufficient funds from depositors to meet the demands of potential borrowers. Not only may banks be fully loaned up in these circumstances, but they may actually seek to borrow additional funds from the central bank. In so doing, of course, they must weigh the cost of such borrowing against the return obtained from its lending operations. In this case, banks will appear to lend more than is allowed by the required reserve ratio and hence the g coefficient will be larger than $1-r$, producing a larger coefficient of multiple expansion.

There is an additional implication of the above analysis worth noting. Even in the absence of reserve requirements, banks will wish to hold idle resources, committing only a part of their assets to loans. Part of the reasoning behind this action is related to our previous arguments. However, it is probably best understood by thinking of the bank, or rather its managers, as having preferences as to its asset and liability structure. Basically there would be three factors influencing an individual bank's attitude towards holding reserves.

(1) At any particular point of time a bank's deposit receipts may not equal withdrawals. While no particular problem arises if there is a net inflow of funds, a very difficult situation would arise if the bank's customers wanted to withdraw funds but there were none available to meet the demand. Thus, even in the absence of reserve requirements,

idle balances will be held by banks. The greater the probability of large withdrawals, the greater will the desired level of reserves be.

(2) But this will not be the only determinant. *Ceteris paribus*, the higher the return to be obtained from loans, the greater the opportunity cost of holding idle funds. Hence one would expect banks to reduce their reserves in the face of higher interest rates.

(3) *Ceteris paribus*, the greater the level of risk associated with potential borrowers, the more reluctant will banks be to loan out funds, that is they would rather hold idle balances.

The above reasoning implies that reserve requirements place a restriction on the expansion of bank deposits, but are not the sole determinant. Even if such requirements were non-existent there would not be an infinite expansion of bank deposits as a mechanical application of the coefficient of multiple expansion would seem to imply. Rather the liquidity requirements and expectations of bank managers with respect to risk and return would be the predominant factors influencing the expansion process.

If the above analysis had been appreciated by more economists, we would probably not have been faced with some of the misleading interpretations placed on activity in the euro-currency system. As it is, it is possible to identify six different descriptions of the multiple expansion process as it might occur in the system. However, such ambiguities and misconceptions are easily forgiven. The growth of the euro-currency system has really been too recent to permit a full understanding of its workings. This is largely due to the unavailability of sufficient data to trace through the intricate linkages between domestic financial markets and the international flow of funds.

Now let us examine the controversies surrounding the various descriptions of the euro-currency multiple expansion process.

Process I

Perhaps the multiplier which has attracted the most attention is the one associated with Milton Friedman,[8] although it has been widely discussed by many others. According to Friedman the key to understanding the euro-currency system lies in the fact that euro-banks are part of a fractional reserve system. Thus he argues that the expansion of euro-currency deposits can be explained by a process completely analogous to the one for ordinary commercial banks as discussed above.

For example, consider the following situation. As we showed in Chapter 2, when a euro-currency deposit is created, the euro-bank obtains a foreign-currency asset. Until the 1970s euro-banks were not, in general, subject to statutory reserve requirements; nevertheless, a proportion of their assets might still be held as reserves, with the remainder lent out. Thus, in the case of our fictitious country, Europa, a bank there might loan out 90 per cent of its dollar assets. The borrower, say Company X, proceeds to purchase goods from Company Y which then redeposits a proportion of the dollars, say 90 per cent, with another euro-bank. The latter then lends 90 per cent of such deposits to Z, goods are purchased from W, and 90 per cent of these receipts are redeposited in the euro-currency system. If carried out through an infinite number of steps, this multiple expansion process appears to be formally identical to the one used to describe domestic deposit creation. With reserve and leakage ratios both 10 per cent, then the euro-currency multiplier can be calculated from equation (6.4) as 5·26. The only difference is that 'reserves' are held at an American commercial bank rather than with a central bank.

There is little doubt that there is some relevance to this analogy. However, it is highly unlikely that the multiplier will be as high as the one in the above examples. To understand this let us consider factors affecting the reserve and leakage ratios characterising the system.

Reserve ratios. There seems to be general agreement that the proportion of euro-bank assets held as reserves is likely to be small. As Klopstock[9] has pointed out, there are several reasons for this. First, a large proportion of euro-currency deposits are payable only at a stated maturity date or after advance notice. Thus the possibility of unforeseen withdrawal is nil, and banks have no need to maintain liquid balances against these liabilities. However, some deposits can be withdrawn upon demand. But even in this case, actual reserves held at an American bank can be kept to a minimum. For one thing, local-currency reserves can be converted into dollars or some other currency should the need arise. In addition, a euro-bank can also borrow funds from another euro-bank or from its correspondents in America or elsewhere. In other words, if it is short of funds it can simply borrow them.

Leakages. On the basis of the above reasoning it would appear that there exists considerable potential for a large expansion of euro-currency deposits if we apply the textbook multiplier in a mechanical fashion. This would appear to be the line taken by Friedman when he writes that the major source of euro-dollars is the 'book-keeper's pen'. In the above example, a proportion of any euro-currency deposit is lent out, thereby creating an additional deposit. However, as Klopstock has argued,[10] only a *small* proportion of these funds will return to the euro-currency system. There are several possibilities. The recipient of the dollar funds may purchase goods in America, in which case they will be deposited in a bank there. This does not involve any change in the reserve position of American banks and brings any expansion of euro-dollar deposits to a complete halt. Another possibility is that the ultimate recipient will convert the dollars received into his own currency, possibly to use the proceeds to pay his own debts. And again the euro-dollar expansion has come to a halt.

One argument justifying the existence of the euro-currency multiplier hinges on the widespread use of these facilities by multinational corporations. However, as Mayer has pointed out, 'there is no reason to assume that these funds are primarily employed for making payments to other large international corporations'.[11] Unfortunately, there currently is not sufficient data available to determine just how important such flows are likely to be.

Process II

In the previous case it was assumed that all loans were made to non-banks. However, it is also possible that euro-banks may place their dollar assets with other euro-banks. This raises the possibility of a 'pyramiding' chain of inter-bank deposits being created. For example, consider Table 6.2. Without worrying about the source of the initial

TABLE 6.2

European Bank B		European Bank C	
Assets	Liabilities	Assets	Liabilities
+ $24 reserves	+ $240 euro-currency deposit	+ $21·60 reserves	+ $216 loan from European Bank B
+ $216 loan to European Bank C		+ $204·40 loan to X	

American Bank A	
Assets	Liabilities
+ $240 reserves	+ $24 deposit of European Bank B
	+ $21·60 deposit of European Bank C
	+ $204·40 deposit of X

deposit, we note that European Bank B has received a euro-currency deposit worth 240 dollars, part of which it holds in the form of reserves at Bank A in America, and part of which it loans to Bank C. For reasons to be discussed, this is made profitable by the fact that C will be offering a higher yield to Bank B than the latter is paying to its depositors. Bank C might then loan the dollar funds so received to another euro-bank and so the process might continue. However, in Table 6.2 I have assumed that Bank C has lent the funds to a non-bank X who thereby obtains claims over funds in America. This brings the inter-bank expansion process to a halt.

In order to understand how pyramiding evolves we must look more carefully at the preferences of non-bank borrowers and lenders. Suppose that lenders have a very strong preference for keeping funds liquid, whereas borrowers want to obtain funds for a longer period of time. Under these circumstances it is likely that an accommodation could be reached, but only at a very high (perhaps prohibitively so) interest rate. However, as we have already argued, this situation provides an opportunity for a financial institution to step in and act as a middleman or intermediary. By taking advantage of the fact that there may be a stable, offsetting pattern of deposits and withdrawals, the financial institution can afford to offer deposits to potential customers without any restrictions on the timing or amounts of any withdrawals. At the same time, because it knows that the total amount of its liabilities are reasonably stable over time, the financial institution can afford to make loans for reasonably long periods of time, charging any borrowers a higher rate of interest than it is paying to its depositors.

However, it is quite possible that several financial intermediaries may become involved, depending on the preferences of various institutions with respect to their asset and liability structure. For example, the bank referred to above may not want to lend funds for the time period desired by the borrowers. However, the bank could lend the funds to another institution which was willing to commit itself for the requisite period of time. The ultimate limit to the number of banks involved will depend on the costs associated with each stage of the intermediary process. The higher the costs, the more must be the spread between the deposit and lending rates for each bank and hence the fewer intermediaries between the initial lender and ultimate borrower. In addition, each loan will have a certain risk attached to it. As the chain lengthens, smaller, perhaps less credit-worthy banks will become involved since these are the only ones willing to pay high interest rates. At some point, however, there will be no other financial institutions willing to pay the high charges necessary to continue the chain. Several implications of this particular expansion process warrant comment.

(i) Each bank in the chain may hold a proportion of its assets as reserves, although as we argued previously it will want to keep this amount as small as possible in order to maximise its profits. Nevertheless, the propensity to hold reserves means that, as the chain of inter-bank deposits gets longer and longer, each succeeding inter-bank loan gets smaller and smaller. Ultimately, this chain will be broken and a loan will be made to a non-bank. However, the longer the chain, the smaller will be the ultimate size of the loan, and hence the less the impact on real economic activity. This is in contrast to Process I where each successive loan was made to a non-bank and hence led to increased purchasing power and output.

(ii) On the basis of our reasoning earlier in this section, the longer the chain of inter-bank deposits, the longer will be the maturity and/or the greater will be the risk associated with each succeeding deposit. But this means that we have a very liquid bank liability, the initial euro-currency deposit, supporting increasingly more illiquid assets. During 'normal' times, no difficulty would appear to be involved. However, given a second glance, it is seen that the system is really balancing on a knife-edge. For example, should euro-currency rates fall significantly below those available in domestic financial markets, a rapid withdrawal of funds from the system will occur. In order to meet the demands of depositors banks will have to sell off some of their assets. The most liquid ones will go first, but if the run on the funds should continue, ultimately the less-marketable assets will have to be disposed of, quite possibly at a loss. If the magnitude of these events should be quite large, the actual day-to-day operations of the bank may be threatened and ultimately bankruptcy may occur.

It should be emphasised that financial institutions participating in the euro-currency system operate in a different environment than do those banks, the bulk of whose business is domestic. In most countries the latter have access to a central bank, which functions as lender of last resort. During difficult periods when a bank may be temporarily short of funds it can seek to borrow funds from the central bank. However, this opportunity is generally not available to euro-banks. There is at the moment no formal lender of last resort in the system. Hence the possibility of bank failure or bankruptcy is considerably greater.

Despite the potential for instability in the euro-currency system, the process of pyramiding, in normal times, tends to improve the allocational efficiency of the international economy. In the absence of the sort of financial intermediation described, it is clear that the wants of deficit and surplus units could be accommodated only at great cost. In the first instance, banks possessing excess funds would have to expend considerable effort searching for potential borrowers. In the second case, it could be difficult to reconcile the preferences of lenders with respect to maturity, risk and return with the needs of borrowers unless several rounds of intermediation were to take place. In the last analysis, it must increase the number of real international transactions, and hence real output, over what otherwise would have taken place.

Process III

Alexander Swoboda[12] has linked the two expansion processes discussed above in an attempt to derive a more general multiplier for the euro-currency system. Suppose that there is a deposit of $100 in the euro-dollar account and that all banks loan out a percentage of their assets so obtained. Then the total amount of inter-bank pyramiding which can take place between the original lender and ultimate borrower is

$$100(1 + b + b^2 + \ldots + b^m),$$

where m denotes the total number of intermediaries involved. The amount $100b^m$ is then lent to a non-bank customer by the last euro-bank in the chain.

Following Swoboda, let us now assume that a proportion d ends up being redeposited in the euro-dollar system, that is there is a new non-bank deposit of $100db^m$. This, in turn, generates inter-bank pyramiding equivalent to

$$(100db^m)(1 + b + b^2 + \ldots + b^m).$$

Another loan, this one worth $100d(b^m)^2$, is made to another non-bank customer and again a proportion d is redeposited in the euro-dollar system by a non-bank customer. The new deposit thus equals $100(db^m)^2$. And so the process continues. On the basis of our earlier analysis of euro-dollar deposits the process can then be described by the series

$$100\,[1 + b^m d + (b^m d)^2 + \ldots + (b^m d)^n],$$

where n, the number of redeposit cycles, approaches infinity. This geometric series equals

$$\frac{1}{1 - b^m d},$$

which is Swoboda's coefficient of multiple expansion associated with the euro-currency system.

While the above device has a good deal of pedagogic value in pointing up the complexities of the system, there are, however, many 'slips 'twixt cup and lip' which need to be emphasised again.

(1) The length of each inter-bank pyramiding chain may not always involve m banks. This number depends on the cost of intermediation at each stage and the spread in the interest paid to each initial depositor and charge to each final lender. This spread, of course, may vary from round to round of the expansion process depending on the type of deposits and loans made. Thus m itself, together with the resulting non-bank loan, will be variable from round to round. The larger is m, that is the longer the pyramid chain, then the smaller is the coefficient.

(2) The proportion of each such deposit held as reserves may be different at each stage of the chain depending upon the asset–liability preferences of each bank.

(3) Likewise the proportion of each non-bank loan which is re-deposited in the euro-currency system may vary at each stage of the expansion, depending upon the portfolio preferences of each potential depositor. Indeed, at any stage, the process may come to a complete halt if a decision is made to deposit funds outside the euro-currency system.

Process IV

Our previous discussion has emphasised a fairly simple two-stage process of expansion concentrating on euro-bank lending procedures and the possibility of subsequent redepositing. Mayer, however, has offered another explanation which at first glance appears different from the processes described so far. He writes that

> for a multiplier to exist it is by no means necessary to assume that the proceeds from the Euro-dollar credits are used only for payments to residents of the reporting European area, or that the dollars are directly redeposited with Euro-banks ... it is quite possible that the dollar proceeds are first converted into national currency and are switched back into dollars and placed at some later stage of the induced income circulation. Leaving aside for the moment the role of monetary authorities and certain other qualifications, all that is necessary for a multiplier effect to exist, however small it may be, is that the Euro-dollar credits add on a worldwide basis to aggregate demand and income circulation and that part of this increased income circulation be reflected in increased current-account balances with the Euro-dollar banks themselves.[13]

Obviously Mayer is thinking of a very general analytical framework describing domestic and international financial flows. However, a simple example will establish what is involved. Suppose that a euro-dollar deposit is created as in our earlier example when a European exporter transfers dollar balances from an American bank to a euro-bank. The latter then sells the acquired dollars for deneros which it lends to a European resident, who in turn purchases goods on the home market. While the firm selling these items might place the bulk of his funds in a denero deposit, part may be exchanged for dollars and placed back in the euro-currency system. Obviously this is a sequence that is unlikely to arise when the transactions involved are only small in size. Rather, it will most likely occur in the case of large multinational corporations. But this process does not require that one corporation use funds from its euro-dollar deposit to pay another corporation which then places the funds in its euro-dollar deposit. The linkage described by Mayer is indirect.

However, this description is only part of the picture. We must also consider what is happening in America. When the euro-bank sells its dollar assets in the initial stages of the above example, there will be a fall in the liabilities and hence reserves held by the American banking system. This, in turn, will set in motion a process of credit contraction. Now, if some American firms had made a practice of depositing funds in the euro-currency system, any reduction in their sales may lead them to draw down on such deposits. Thus the events leading up to an increase in euro-currency deposits held by Europeans may also set in motion a reduction in such deposits held by Americans. This is a point which Mayer appears to have neglected. However, he is correct in calling our attention to the need for studying more closely the relationship between international and domestic flows of funds.

Process V

An entirely different sort of explanation of the euro-currency system has been offered by Clendenning.[14] As we shall see in the next chapter, an early and continuing source of funds to the system has been central banks seeking to obtain the highest possible return on their international reserves. Clendenning has argued that this motivation has led to a process involving a continuous redepositing of funds and generation of bank credit. For example, suppose that the euro-bank takes a proportion g of the funds obtained from any newly acquired euro-dollar deposit and uses them to purchase deneros. If euro-dollar reserve and private sector redeposit ratios are both zero and if nothing further were to occur, the central bank would intervene to purchase the dollars in order to maintain a fixed exchange rate. Europa would have a balance-of-payments surplus as well as an increase in its money supply. However, now suppose that the European central bank deposits a proportion k of its newly acquired dollar reserves back in the euro-currency system. This would then set in motion another round of similar events, with the result that a given dollar deposit of an American bank could be passed back and forth between the euro-bank and the European central bank.

This provides a basis for deriving a euro-currency multiplier as follows. Let D represent the initial euro-dollar deposit, as in our previous examples. The euro-bank sells gD of this for deneros which in turn leads the European central bank to increase its euro-dollar holdings by kgD. The second-round deposit is kg^2D, and so forth *ad infinitum*. The total change in euro-dollar deposits can then be written as a geometric series of the form

$$\text{T.D.} = D(1 + kg + kg^2 + \ldots + kg^n),$$

which in turn can be shown to equal

$$D\left(\frac{1}{1-kg}\right).$$

As with the parameters discussed in the other sections of this chapter, neither k nor g can be expected to remain constant over time. The higher euro-currency interest rates are compared to those available elsewhere, the higher will be the proportion of reserve assets placed by central banks in the system. And the higher are interest rates available on domestic assets, the higher will be the proportion of euro-currency liabilities sold by euro-banks on the foreign-exchange market. Thus the higher are k and g, the greater the above multiplier will be; the lower they are, the closer to zero will be this multiplier. If both k and g were equal to one, the multiplier would be infinity!

It should also be noted that if the euro-currency system did not exist, then the international-liquidity position of Europa would equal the sum of previous balance-of-payments surpluses with America minus any deficits, where these figures are on the official settlements basis. However, when dollars obtained by a euro-bank are sold and then redeposited in the system by the European central bank, this is no longer the case. The euro-bank disposes of one dollar asset but immediately obtains another. Both will be equal if the parameter g equals 1. Yet there has been no balance-of-payments deficit in America although Europa's dollar reserves would appear to rise. As a result we can write

$$R_E = R_{ED} + BUS,$$

where R_E is the European central bank's total reserve position, R_{ED} its euro-dollar holdings and BUS the net sum of balance-of-payments surpluses and deficits with America.

However, a word of warning is in order. While strictly correct from an accounting viewpoint, including a central bank's euro-dollar deposits may actually lead to an overstatement of its international-liquidity position. For example, suppose Europa suffers a payments deficit and that it uses dollars deposited with euro-banks to maintain a fixed exchange rate with America. But in order to meet these withdrawals, the euro-bank must sell off some of its denero assets, further adding to the excess supply of deneros on the foreign-exchange market and to Europa's balance-of-payments deficit. The central bank must increase its intervention. Whereas a multiplier was previously used to explain the expansion of the system, it must now also be used to explain its contraction. In other words, the initial withdrawal of euro-dollars by the central bank sets in motion a sequence of events which places additional demands on its international reserves.

Process VI

Perhaps the most interesting attempt to explain the expansion of the euro-currency system has been provided by Hewson and Sakakibara.[15] All of the processes described so far in this chapter have assumed fixed parameters, although we have argued that in reality this is not likely to be the case. Hewson and Sakakibara, recognising this, offer an analytical framework which attempts to take into account the portfolio behaviour of euro-currency borrowers and lenders. A simple example, based on their analysis, will illustrate what is involved. Suppose again that there is a shift of funds from America to a euro-dollar deposit located at a bank in Europa. In addition, assume that domestic market interest rates remain constant in both countries, although euro-dollar rates are free to vary so that the demand for euro-dollar deposits and the supply of euro-dollar loans are always equal. It is assumed that no dollar assets are converted to deneros. This implies the equilibrium condition

$$\sum_{i}^{2} D_i = \sum_{i}^{2} L_i,$$

(6.5)

where D_i is the demand for euro-dollar deposits by residents of country i, and L_i is the demand for euro-dollar loans by residents of country i. In addition, assume that D_i and L_i respond to changes in euro-dollar rates such that

$$D_i = \lambda_i + b_i r_{ED}$$

(6.6)

and

$$L_i = \theta_i + d_i r_{ED},$$

(6.7)

where $b_i > 0$ and $d_i < 0$. We shall also assume that $\lambda_i > 0$ and $\theta_i > 0$.

The effect of the exogenous shift in dollar funds, $\triangle \lambda$, from an American bank to a euro-bank is to shift the demand curve to the left; this is equivalent to an increase in the intercept of Europa's demand function for euro-dollars. Substituting equations (6.6) and (6.7) into equation (6.5) and then rearranging terms, we can obtain an expression for changes in r_{ED} in terms of $\triangle \lambda$, such that

$$\frac{\triangle r_{ED}}{\triangle \lambda} = \frac{1}{\sum(d_i - b_i)}.$$

(6.8)

This expresses the change in the euro-dollar rate necessary to clear the system following an exogenous change in demand for euro-dollar deposits.

The change in the total size of the system, $\triangle S$, can be written in the form of a multiplier as follows:

$$\frac{\triangle S}{\triangle \lambda} = \frac{\triangle \lambda + \sum \triangle D_i}{\triangle \lambda} = 1 + \left(\frac{\sum \triangle D_i}{\triangle r_{ED}}\right)\left(\frac{\triangle r_{ED}}{\triangle \lambda}\right),$$

(6.9)

which, upon substitution of equation (6.8), equals

$$1 + \frac{\sum b_i}{\sum(d_i - b_i)}.$$

This multiplier is positive but must be less than one.

If we allow for balance-of-payments and central-bank deposits in the system, the upper limit for the multiplier will be higher. Given the decrease in interest rates which will occur because of the exogenous increase in euro-dollar deposits, savers will transfer some funds to deneros. This gives rise to balance-of-payments surplus for Europa and raises the possibility that the European central bank may wish to deposit part of its funds in the system. Allowing for this possibility, Hewson and Sakakibara *estimate* that the multiplier should be, at most, 1·4. This is marginally higher than the multiplier of 1·05 to 1·09 calculated by Mayer[16] by interpreting a widely quoted comment by Klopstock.[17]

SUMMARY

We have shown that while there is potentially an analogy between the multiple expansion process describing domestic bank behaviour and the growth of the euro-currency system, it is bound to be misleading. For one thing, while euro-banks are not likely to hold a high proportion of their assets as reserves (unless legally required to do so), the redeposit ratio characterising the system is likely to be low. Further, these proportions are likely to be variables themselves: a proper understanding of the system can only be obtained by examining it within the framework of portfolio analysis, in a fashion similar to that of Hewson and Sakakibara.[18] Finally, the potential role of central banks in expanding the system is quite important, as we shall see in the following two chapters.

FURTHER READING

E. W. Clendenning, 'Euro-Dollars and Credit Creation', *International Currency Review*, 3 (Mar–Apr 1971).

Milton Friedman, 'The Euro-Dollar Market: Some First Principles', *Morgan Guaranty Survey* (Oct 1969); reprinted in *Review of the Federal Reserve Bank of St Louis*, 53 (July 1971).

J. Hewson and E. Sakakibara, 'The Euro-Dollar Deposit Multiplier: A Portfolio Approach', *International Monetary Fund Staff Papers*, 22 (Mar 1975).

F. H. Klopstock, *The Euro-Dollar Market: Some Unresolved Issues*, Essays in International Finance, no. 65 (Princeton University, Mar 1968).

F. H. Klopstock, 'Money Creation in the Euro-Dollar Market – A Note on Professor Friedman's Views', *Review of the Federal Reserve Bank of New York*, 52 (Jan 1970).

F. Machlup, 'Euro-Dollar Creation: A Mystery Story', *Banca del Lavoro Quarterly Review* (Sep 1970).

H. Mayer, 'Multiplier Effects and Credit Creations in the Euro-Dollar Market', *Banca del Lavoro Quarterly Review* (Sep 1971).

A. K. Swoboda, *The Euro-Dollar Market: An Interpretation*, Essays in International Finance, no. 64 (Princeton University, Feb 1968).

J. Tobin, 'Commercial Banks as Creators of "Money"', in *Banking and Monetary Studies*, ed. D. Carson (Homewood, Ill.: Irwin, 1963).

7

Development and Growth of the Euro-Currency System: The Formative Years, 1958–69

The tendency of most observers has been to trace the development of the euro-currency system to a specific event or set of circumstances which appeared to act as a spark encouraging the practice of banks accepting deposits denominated in foreign currencies. In my own view, the main causes of the rapid and continuous growth have been the often unrelated policy measures adopted by many central banks to control their international *and* domestic financial positions. With each event further impetus was given to the system and, as operators became more familiar with its potential, further growth occurred.

In many ways there is no such thing as a new idea or discovery. Most advances whether social or purely scientific are really based on previous 'discoveries' and merely incorporate some small change or slight twist.* Such is the case of the euro-currency system. Paul Einzig in his *History of Foreign Exchange* has traced the type of activity characterising the system back to medieval times.[2] Then it was frequently the practice at quarterly fairs to draw bills payable in terms of currencies other than that of the country in which the fair was being held. Prior to the Second World War, several European banks did accept deposits denominated in dollars, but the practice was not widespread and the funds thus obtained were reinvested in U.S. financial markets. In contrast, banks operating in the euro-currency system today find wide use for their dollar funds outside the United States. Altman points to the practice of Eastern European banks of depositing their dollar funds not with U.S. banks but with banks located in Europe.[3] This was done presumably to conceal from U.S. authorities the extent of their dollar holdings and to avoid the possibility that these assets would be expropriated.

The most significant turning point, however, occurred in 1957. Prior to that date, European banks had simply followed the pre-1939 practice of reinvesting their dollar funds in the United States. However, in that year the Bank of England placed restrictions on the granting of sterling credits with a view to limiting the availability of the funds for speculation. At the time the expectation was that the pound would be devalued, and hence there was an incentive for foreign traders to increase

---

* There is at present no general theory of financial innovation. However, a start in this direction has been made by Silber.[1]

their sterling liabilities. If the devaluation occurred as forecast (which it did not in this case), the speculators would repay the loan but with fewer units of their own currency. Restricted in the amount of sterling trade credits which they could grant, U.K. banks then resorted to lending dollars to those traders who otherwise would have purchased pounds. And these traders were not necessarily Americans, but Europeans. For the first time dollar assets were widely placed outside the United States.

A crucial element in the system taking root was that the U.S. dollar was ideally suited as a vehicle currency. As Swoboda has shown,[4] the transactions costs associated with the dollar are extremely low, an important condition for it to fulfil the role of a vehicle. In addition it is widely accepted throughout the international economy. It is backed by a stable political system and until recently has had a stable exchange rate against other currencies. It also has a broad market, largely as a result of the importance of the United States as an international trader and financial centre and the financial expertise of New York banking institutions. Its attractiveness was further enhanced by the return to exchange-rate convertibility in 1958 and the fact that the dollar was subject to few exchange controls. Indeed, the role of the dollar had been institutionalised in the Articles of Agreement of the I.M.F. which allowed countries to state their exchange rates either per ounce of gold or in terms of the dollar.

THE ROLE OF CENTRAL BANKS

Statistics on the size and make-up of the euro-currency system are to-day woefully lacking. In the early 1960s they were virtually non-existent. However, it is possible to piece together a picture of its early growth based on the statements of various observers and official institutions. Oscar Altman of the I.M.F. estimated that from the end of 1960 to the end of 1962, *total* euro-dollar deposits grew from about 2000 million to over 5000 million.[5] Of this amount he estimated that about two-thirds represents deposits made directly through central banks or indirectly through the auspices of the Bank for International Settlements (B.I.S.).* The remainder represented deposits owned by commercial banks and by various business enterprises including foreign

---

* The Bank for International Settlements has frequently been neglected in discussions of the international monetary system. Briefly, it was set up following the First World War to administer reparations payments. Following the Second World War it became the agent of the European Payments Union whose task was to help countries organise their balance of international payments in the absence of currency convertibility. Recently it has played an important role in the international monetary system by stabilising exchange rates in general and the euro-currency system in particular. For a more detailed discussion of the Bank's activities, see Schloss.[6]

traders. Einzig[7] holds that this figure represents an overstatement although he does not deny the considerable impact of central-bank deposits. Evidence as to the magnitude of this role is also offered in the 1963–4 Annual Report of the B.I.S. They note this action by several central banks in Europe and elsewhere, pointing out that in a few of the cases such deposits were in the range of $200 to $300 million.

Since central-bank deposits continue to provide a substantial source of growth for the euro-currency system, it is important to examine the various reasons for such activity in detail. Basically there are three motivations:

(a) Certain central banks have used the euro-currency system to obtain the highest return possible on their international reserves;

(b) They have engaged in various operations involving euro-currency deposits designed to affect the liquidity position of their own commercial banks and ultimately their money supply; and

(c) They have attempted to stabilise the system by offsetting certain year-end balance-sheet operations ('window dressing') by euro-banks through the use of swap arrangements.

Let us examine each of these points in turn.

(a) Maximisation of return on international reserves

The central-bank practice of depositing funds in the euro-currency system appeared to develop in 1960 and 1961 when interest rates in the United States were considerably lower than those available on euro-dollar deposits. Over this period, the interest on three-month bank deposits was 2·5 per cent whereas that paid on euro-dollar deposits fluctuated roughly between 3·5 and 4 per cent. The main reason for this spread was the existence of Regulation Q imposed by the Federal Reserve Board and limiting the interest rates that commercial banks could pay. This regulation was subsequently amended by the U.S. Congress in 1962 so as to exempt interest rates paid on time deposits held by foreign *official* institutions.

In many ways the implications of such euro-currency deposits by central banks are similar to those arising when any individual possessing dollars decides to redeposit them with a euro-bank (see Situation III in Chapter 2). Suppose that the central bank is holding a time deposit at a U.S. commercial bank. If it withdraws the funds and redeposits them with a euro-bank, there is no net change in the position of the U.S. bank, simply a change in deposit ownership. The euro-bank, however, has additional resources. There is no change in either country's international reserve position.

The outcome is different, however, if the original dollar deposit was held with the Federal Reserve System and not a commercial bank. Consider Table 7.1. The funds withdrawn from the Federal Reserve lead to an increase in dollar liabilities and assets at the euro-bank. In turn, the latter's deposit with U.S. Bank A leads to an increase in U.S. bank reserves and an ultimate expansion in loans and demand deposits held by non-banks. In other words, there will have been an increase in liquidity at both the euro-bank and U.S. Bank A. The international

TABLE 7.1

Federal Reserve System		Euro-bank	
Assets	*Liabilities*	*Assets*	*Liabilities*
	− $100 deposit of European central bank	deposit at U.S. correspondent Bank A + $100	deposit of European central bank + $100
	+ $100 reserves of U.S. Bank A		

U.S. Bank A		European Central Bank	
Assets	*Liabilities*	*Assets*	*Liabilities*
reserves held with F.R.S. + $100	deposit of euro-bank + $100	deposit with F.R.S. − $100	
		deposit at euro-bank + $100	

reserve position of the European central bank remains unchanged, since it will include its euro-dollar deposits in this figure. However, the international reserve position of the Federal Reserve has improved since its liabilities to foreign central banks have declined. Its net liability position, on the other hand, is unchanged since commercial-bank reserves have increased.

Central banks can also utilise the facilities of the Bank for International Settlements in order to participate in the euro-currency system. This enables them to obtain the higher return required and at the same time preserve their anonymity since the B.I.S. does not publish detailed accounts. However, they do publish condensed asset and liability statements. Of particular interest is the fact that its time-deposit placements increased from 454 million Swiss francs in 1960 to 8964 million in 1969, as shown in Table 7.2. A large part of this 17-fold increase must have represented deposits in the euro-currency system placed on behalf of central banks.[8] The implications of this intermediation are really no different from those involved in direct placements by central

banks. The only change is that the central bank holds a deposit at the
B.I.S. which in turn holds a deposit at a euro-bank.

TABLE 7.2

Time deposits and advances
held by the
Bank for International Settlements

(*Millions of Swiss francs
as of 31 March*)

1960	454	1965	2191
1961	1138	1966	2507
1962	1294	1967	3551
1963	1245	1968	5775
1964	1594	1969	8964

SOURCE: Bank for International Settlements,
Annual Reports.

The Friedman–Klopstock debate. Over the years it has frequently been
argued in both official and academic circles that the main source of
funds to the euro-currency system has been the U.S. balance-of-payments deficit. This issue arose again in the debate between Friedman
and Klopstock, and has not entirely been clarified. Since the resolution
of this discussion hinges on the material which has just been covered in
this chapter, it is convenient to take a short digression at this juncture.

Friedman has taken the position that the U.S. balance of payments
is not a sufficient condition for the growth of the system. He writes that
'Balance-of-payments deficits do provide foreigners with claims on U.S.
dollars. But there is nothing to assure that claims will be held in the
form of Euro-dollars.'[9] As we have noted foreigners may wish to hold
dollar assets either as working balances (that is as a vehicle currency)
or because they yield a higher return than other investment instruments. And these same foreigners may wish to hold part of these dollar
assets with euro-banks because it is more convenient to do so and/or
because they offer a higher return than available on similar deposits in
the United States. However, this situation could arise even if the United
States had a payments surplus. Consider the case of West Germany
which has surpluses, and yet euro-mark deposits have shown considerable growth. Conversely, even given a U.S. deficit, there is no inherent
reason why foreigners should hold dollars at all. If it is no longer
attractive as a vehicle currency or for investment purposes, any dollar
holdings can simply be exchanged for similar assets denominated in
another currency.

On the other hand, there is also support for Klopstock's view that the
U.S. balance of payments has been an important source of funds to the

euro-currency system. However, in this instance the source is not private firms and individuals, as Friedman seems to imply, but central banks. This is a point partly clarified by Klopstock in a reply to Friedman:

> As foreign banks and non-banks convert their own currencies into dollars in order to be able to make deposits with Euro-banks, and as central banks place monetary reserves in the market, they draw on dollars currently or previously accumulated abroad in consequence of our balance-of-payments deficits. In this particular sense, those who argue that the source of Euro-dollar deposits is 'partly U.S. balance-of-payments deficits' and 'partly dollar reserves of non-U.S. central banks' are correct.[10]

Klopstock's comment represents only a partial clarification since foreign banks and non-banks do not necessarily have to draw upon dollars previously accumulated. Rather they can simply purchase the dollars at the same time that they deposit them with a euro-bank. And this action could occur even if the United States were in surplus. On the other hand, to the extent that central banks have accumulated dollars as a result of a U.S. payments deficit and then depositing them in the euro-currency system, Klopstock's remarks are correct.

(b) Role in monetary policy

In any textbook dealing with financial institutions and monetary policy, an important place is usually given to the role of open-market operations as an instrument for domestic stabilisation. For example, consider the sale of U.S. Treasury securities by the Federal Reserve. Deposits of security dealers fall, thus producing a reduction in bank loans and hence a slowing down in economic activity. However, such action in the securities market is only possible in countries like the United States where there exist financial instruments, such as Treasury securities, which are widely held and broadly acceptable.

In countries where open-market operations are not likely to be successful, other techniques must be found if bank liquidity is to be controlled. One particular procedure, widely used in Italy and frequently in West Germany, involves operations in the foreign-exchange markets. One particular technique is the negotiation of swap arrangements by the central bank of the country concerned with their commercial banks. The monetary authorities sell their holdings of foreign currency to the commercial banks under the understanding that they will be repurchased at a specified exchange rate. In other words, the banks are provided with forward cover, usually at a rate designed to make the transaction highly desirable. The commercial banks in turn agree to purchase foreign assets with these funds.

An interesting example of this operation is provided by the case of West Germany in the late 1950s and early 1960s. Over this period, the German balance of payments was consistently in surplus. As we saw in Chapter 2 this can lead to an increase in cash balance in German banks and hence stimulate an increase in economic activity. However, at the time the German economy was already booming and hence the increased bank reserves had to be neutralised. This was done using swap arrangements as described above. Over the years the banks were offered a wide variety of maturities ranging from a period of two weeks to one of six months. During the period, the maximum level of outstanding swaps occurred in October 1962 when they stood at more than one billion dollars.

In contrast the Italian central bank has deposited foreign currency with its banks without any restrictions. For example, this was done in 1959 in order to expand bank liquidity. The commercial banks were then able to sell the dollars for lire (and thus were able to expand their loans) or they bought foreign assets. In the latter case the expansion was indirect. If the foreign assets had been purchased from an Italian, then he would have exchanged the foreign currency received for lire before bank liquidity was affected.

(c) Exchange-rate stabilisation

At the end of the year, those banks with substantial assets and liabilities in foreign currency engage in what are called 'window-dressing' operations. In other words, they attempt to bring their asset and liability positions into line thereby eliminating any open positions. As Kindleberger has pointed out,[11] this activity does not fool anyone. However, it has brought substantial pressure to bear on foreign-currency markets and the euro-currency system in particular. In the course of 'window dressing' the banks have sold off their dollar assets, in turn putting pressures on the dollar exchange rate. In addition, this activity has reduced the supply of funds in the euro-dollar system. An example of this seasonal pattern occurred on 29 November 1966 when the one-month euro-dollar rate was pushed up from $6\frac{1}{2}$ per cent to $7\frac{3}{8}$ per cent. In response, the authorities undertook a multi-pronged attack which became a model for future responses to exchange crises as well as for 'window-dressing' operations.

First, the Swiss National Bank bought 400 million dollars from Swiss commercial banks under a swap contract similar to those discussed in the previous section. These funds were then deposited in the euro-dollar system either directly or through the offices of the B.I.S. In addition, the Swiss National Bank also opened up 75 million dollars of euro-dollar deposits with dollar funds already held as international reserves.

Second, the B.I.S. activated its reciprocal currency arrangement with the Federal Reserve by drawing 200 million dollars. Basically these arrangements involve the creation of bilateral lines of credit. Each partner to an agreement opens up an account in its own currency in the name of the other, with the result that the net asset–liability position of each central bank remains unchanged. When one central bank requires funds for intervention in the foreign-exchange market, it may draw on its account with its partner, although this usually requires prior notification and agreement. In this particular case the B.I.S. drew the funds for channelling into the euro-dollar system.

Finally, action was taken to offset selling pressure on sterling caused by the high rates in the euro-dollar system. The New York Federal Reserve Bank purchased 88 million dollars worth of pounds under one-month swap contracts calling for forward delivery in January 1967. As a result the temporary excess supply of pounds was offset.

Success in stabilising exchange rates and the euro-currency system, not only in the face of seasonal difficulties but also under difficulties such as posed by the Suez crisis, created considerable optimism among central bankers. As Charles Coombs of the New York Federal Reserve wrote in 1968

> as the experience of the last year indicates, the Euro-currency market itself is surprisingly resilient in the face of fairly severe shocks and, so long as national central banks are prepared to cooperate in tempering the pressures to which the market is subjected, the risk of serious repercussions being transmitted by and through the market can be minimized.[12]

INSTITUTIONAL DEVELOPMENTS

One of the most significant influences on the development of the euro-currency system during the 1960s was its use as a source of loanable funds by U.S. commercial banks. In order to understand why this occurred, it is really necessary to view it as part of a series of financial innovations begun by the banks in 1961 and stimulated in part by actions of the Federal Reserve. Between 1945 and 1961 the share of U.S. savings going to commercial banks had fallen from 53·5 per cent to 39·9 per cent. The reasons for this are quite easy to determine. Under Regulation Q, the Federal Reserve set ceilings on the interest payable on time and savings deposits. Until 1957 these were considerably below the amount that could be obtained on similar investments with savings and loan associations. In addition, corporations could not receive interest on savings deposits, and as a matter of policy New York City banks paid no interest at all on commercial time deposits. Thus corporations had the choice of holding funds idle or investing in money-market securities since savings and loan associations were prohibited from even accepting deposits of commercial enterprises.

Concerned about the relative deterioration of the position of commercial banks, the Federal Reserve increased the Regulation Q ceilings in 1957. Then in 1961 New York City banks and large banks in other cities took a positive step forward and began issuing negotiable certificates of deposits (C.D.s). A C.D. is essentially a time deposit which matures after a specified period. However, since it is negotiable (that is there exists a market for C.D.s) it could be sold before maturity should the holder require funds. The result of this innovation was that banks began to recapture their share of savings: this rose from 39·9 per cent in 1961 to 43·8 per cent in 1965 and thence to 47 per cent in 1968. But the issuance of C.D.s had other benefits as well. As funds were transferred from demand deposits to C.D.s, banks obtained additional funds since reserve requirements on the latter are considerably lower than on demand deposits. For example, in 1961 4 per cent of funds generated by time deposits had to be held idle as reserves whereas 16·5 per cent was the requirement against demand deposits. In addition, the existence of C.D.s meant that individual banks could more effectively maintain their share of funds. Previously when corporations withdrew funds from their deposits to buy interest-bearing securities, the seller of the securities would most likely redeposit the money with *another* bank. The original bank would lose reserves.

U.S. commercial banks not only sought to obtain a larger share of available savings but also to make more efficient use of the funds available to them. At any point in time, some banks will possess excess reserves while others will be short. The latter could, of course, try to borrow from the Federal Reserve. However, a more efficient procedure had been developed in the 1930s: banks requiring funds would borrow them from banks with excess reserves. The result was what is now called the 'federal-funds market'. It grew particularly rapidly during the 1960s partly in response to tight monetary policies followed by the Federal Reserve and partly because of the computer-based communications system introduced by the latter. This enables inter-bank transfers to be undertaken swiftly and efficiently.

With the burgeoning of the euro-dollar system an alternative source of bank borrowing became available. When federal-funds interest rates rose above euro-dollar rates, there was an incentive for banks to increase their short-term borrowing from the system and vice versa. Therefore it was to be expected that, during times of credit stringency, U.S. banks, and particularly those with foreign branches, would resort to the euro-dollar system for needed funds. Such a situation began to develop in 1965 when the United States expanded its role in the South-east Asian conflict. Military expenditures rose sharply, pushing the federal budget into deficit. Although the U.S. economy was already fully employed, the Administration decided, at least for the time being, against any major tax increases – partly, no doubt, because it would be politically unpopular. The increased borrowing by the government would alone probably have caused higher interest rates in the United States. However, since the economy was already at full employment, the Federal Reserve undertook a restrictive monetary policy with a view to cooling down inflationary pressures. Interest rates rose dramatically producing what has been called the 'credit crunch'.

While these higher rates would no doubt have encouraged banks to borrow funds abroad either directly or through the euro-currency system, a number of factors added a significant stimulus to such a move. In 1966 and 1968 but particularly during 1969 interest rates on investment instruments such as commercial paper and U.S. Treasury bills rose above the maximum rates allowable for certificates of deposit under Regulation Q. The result was a massive run-off of C.D.s as shown in Figure 7.1. As a result there was a large increase in U.S. bank borrowing

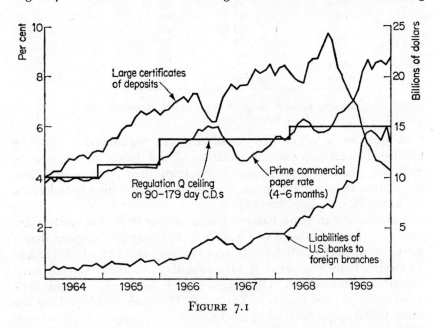

FIGURE 7.1

from their foreign branches as well as an increase in the number of such branches. This latter development has continued unabated ever since (see Table 7.5).

The borrowing from foreign branches was made attractive by the following factors. First, they were not subject to Regulation Q, but

D

rather to the banking practices in the country in which they were domiciled. Thus they could pay whatever was required to obtain funds. But other factors made this activity attractive as well. Under Regulation Q banks could not pay interest on deposits of less than thirty-days maturity. However, on euro-currency deposits such interest could be

TABLE 7.5

Foreign branches of Federal Reserve System member banks

End of year	Number of banks having foreign branches	Number of branches	Number of countries involved
1960	8	124	33
1961	8	135	35
1962	10	145	39
1963	10	160	42
1964	11	180	45
1965	13	211	50
1966	13	244	53
1967	15	295	54
1968	26	373	57
1969	53	459	60
1970	79	532	66
1971	91	577	67
1972	107	627	73
1973	125	699	76

SOURCE: Board of Governors of the Federal Reserve System, *Annual Reports* (1960–73).

paid and thus a whole new set of customer requirements could be fulfilled. In addition, under Regulation M U.S. banks did not have to hold any reserves against borrowing from their foreign branches. Regulation D contained similar exemption for borrowing from foreign banks which were not branches.

The changes in bank balance sheets arising from this activity are similar to those discussed in Chapter 2. For example, suppose that a European exporter moves funds from the head office of a U.S. bank to its foreign branch in order to take advantage of higher interest rates available from the latter. The foreign branch then lends the funds back to its head office as shown in Table 7.6. The bank is able to keep the funds that it might otherwise have lost and, in addition, finds that it can lend the entire amount of its additional liquidity whereas the original deposit of the exporter was subject to a reserve requirement. In addition, the foreign branch may be able to compete funds away from European money markets. In order to obtain dollars, Europeans will sell their own currency depositing the proceeds with the subsidiary. The reader is left to show the balance-sheet implications of this situation.

TABLE 7.6

U.S. Bank *A*		Foreign branch of U.S. Bank *A*	
Assets	*Liabilities*	*Assets*	*Liabilities*
	deposit of European exporter − $100	loan to head office in New York	deposit of European exporter + $100
	loan from foreign branch + $100		

THE EURO-BOND MARKET

Another example of a financial innovation affecting the euro-currency system has been the development of the euro-bond market. Again, official policies were responsible. First, the Bank of England was keen to develop the City of London as an international financial centre. Second, the United States introduced a series of measures designed to improve its balance-of-payments position: an interest-equalisation tax, a voluntary restraint programme and a mandatory foreign-direct-investment programme. Each of these events stimulated the issuing of euro-bonds as opposed to more conventional ways of long-term borrowing.

In October 1962 the Governor of the Bank of England stated that 'The time has now come when the City once again might well provide an international capital market where the foreigner cannot only borrow long-term capital but where, equally important, he will once again wish to place his long-term investment capital.'[13] Six months later, in April 1963, the U.K. government announced measures to make this a reality. Specifically, stamp taxes on stock transfers were lowered, and bearer, as well as registered, securities were allowed to be issued. These measures which became effective in August 1963 provided considerable impetus to the growth of the London capital market.

A further significant stimulus to this expansion came in the form of the U.S. interest-equalisation tax announced in July 1963. Basically this involved a levy placed on purchases of foreign securities and bonds by U.S. residents and was designed to improve the capital account of the U.S. balance of payments. Although it was Americans who in fact paid the tax, the incidence of this action also fell on foreigners who were forced to pay higher interest rates in order to raise funds in the United States. As a result the quantity of foreign bonds issued in New York quickly fell. Prior to this time, bonds were denominated in the currency of the country in which they were floated. With the imposition of the interest-equalisation tax, however, it became advantageous for borrowers to issue bonds in dollars for sale simultaneously in several European financial centres. London, instilled with new life, became the focal point for such euro-bond issues. This technique enabled national restrictions on foreign borrowing in local currencies to be circumvented. At the same time funds could also be mobilised on a European-wide scale whereas conventional issues had been restricted by the ability of single financial centres to absorb many issues.

As can be seen from Table 7.7, Europeans were the main issuers of euro-bonds through the first half of 1965. But in February 1965, the President of the United States announced a programme, largely voluntary in nature, designed to improve the U.S. balance of payments. There were many aspects to the plan. One called upon the Federal Reserve System to work with all banks to limit lending to foreigners.

TABLE 7.7

Euro-bond issues, 1963–9

(millions of dollars)

Country of borrower	1963	1964	1965	1966	1967	1968	1969
United States	—	—	331	439	527	2059	1032
Continental Europe	88	408	456	426	886	658	1082
United Kingdom	—	—	25	40	51	134	235
Japan	20	162	25	—	—	180	246
Canada	—	—	—	—	—	38	228
Rest of World	25	5	83	101	305	259	247
International institutions	5	121	128	101	—	40	40

SOURCE: Bank for International Settlements, *Annual Reports.*

But of more immediate interest to our discussion here, many U.S. corporations were asked to improve their individual international balance-of-payments positions by 15 to 20 per cent. One of the possibilities open to them was increased borrowing abroad, with the result that one-third of the euro-bond issues in 1965 were made by U.S. corporations. And in the process London began to lose some of its business to New York underwriters.

Further impetus to the issuing of euro-bonds by U.S. corporations came on 1 January 1968 with the announcement of mandatory controls on U.S. direct investment abroad. As of that date transfers of U.S. funds for direct investment in most Western European countries were subject to a complete moratorium. In the future, corporations would have to rely on foreign sources and, within limits, on reinvestment of earnings accruing overseas. Thus euro-bond issues by U.S. corporations

grew almost fourfold between 1967 and 1968, although the market con-
tracted somewhat in 1969 as several European countries took steps to
restrict purchases of euro-bonds by domestic residents. These controls
are motivated partly for balance-of-payments reasons and partly because of a fear that the availability of funds to domestic borrowers was
being restricted.

The emergence and rapid growth of the euro-bond market over this
period had two basic implications for the euro-currency system as a
whole. First, it can be viewed as a broadening of the system: euro-
currency deposits are essentially short-term investment vehicles, whereas euro-bonds are long-term. Further, it provided an additional instrument in which euro-banks could invest their funds. Second, there is a
direct link between the euro-bond market and euro-currency deposits.
Inevitably there will be a period of time between the moment when the
issuer of the euro-bonds obtains his funds and when he actually uses
them. During this hiatus, the proceeds will inevitably be deposited in
the euro-currency system until they are required. Thus, at least temporarily, euro-bonds represent another source of liquidity to the system.

FURTHER READING

O. L. Altman, 'Foreign Markets for Dollars, Sterling and Other Currencies',
  International Monetary Fund Staff Papers, 8 (Dec 1961).
O. L. Altman, 'Recent Developments in Foreign Markets for Dollars and
  Other Currencies', in *Factors Affecting the United States Balance of Payments*,
  Joint Economic Committee of the 87th U.S. Congress (Washington: U.S.
  Government Printing Office, 1962).
O. L. Altman, 'Recent Developments in Foreign Markets for Dollars and
  Other Currencies', *International Monetary Fund Staff Papers*, 10 (Mar 1963).
O. L. Altman, 'Euro-Dollars – Some Further Comments', *International
  Monetary Fund Staff Papers*, 12 (Mar 1965).
Bank for International Settlements, *Thirty-Fourth Annual Report* (Basle, 1964).
C. A. Coombs, 'Treasury and Federal Reserve Foreign Exchange
  Operations', *Review of the Federal Reserve Bank of New York* (Mar 1968).
P. Einzig, *The Eurodollar System* (London: Macmillan, 1973).
M. Friedman, 'The Euro-Dollar Market: Some First Principles', *Morgan
  Guaranty Survey* (Oct 1969); reprinted in *Review of the Federal Reserve Bank
  of St Louis* (July 1971).
J. Heinz *et al.*, 'Recent Innovations in European Capital Markets', *Review
  of the Federal Reserve Bank of New York* (Jan 1965).
C. P. Kindleberger, *International Economics*, 5th edn (Homewood, Ill.: Irwin,
  1973).
F. H. Klopstock, 'Money Creation in the Euro-Dollar Market – A Note on
  Professor Friedman's Views', *Review of the Federal Reserve Bank of New York*
  (Jan 1970).

H. H. Schloss, 'The Bank for International Settlements', *Bulletin of the Schools of Business of New York University*, nos 65–6 (Sep 1970).

W. Silber, 'Innovation in the Financial Sector', Working Paper No. 31, Salomon Brothers Center for the Study of Financial Institutions (Mar 1975).

A. Swoboda, 'Vehicle Currencies and the Foreign Exchange Market: The Case of the Dollar', in *The International Market For Foreign Exchange*, ed. Robert E. Aliber (New York: Praeger, 1969).

8

Development and Growth of the Euro-Currency System: The Maturing Years, 1970–4

As we have seen, until 1970 the major factors affecting the development of the euro-currency system had been (*a*) direct intervention by Western European central banks and (*b*) the competitive bidding for funds by the foreign branches of U.S. banks. From 1970 onwards the character of the system changed dramatically. It was dominated by two series of events. First, there was a growing recognition that the pool of funds making up the euro-currency system could render monetary policies ineffective. This became particularly apparent over 1970 and 1971 when the United States was attempting to follow policies of monetary and fiscal ease whereas European countries were still concerned with restraining inflation. The results, as we shall see, were dramatic, bringing to a virtual end the Bretton Woods adjustable-peg exchange-rate system. Second, the euro-currency system became an important depository of funds from those countries producing primary commodities which had been benefiting from higher prices. However, whereas depositors have wanted to hold assets only of short maturity, euro-banks found that they could most profitably lend for long periods of time. And this lengthening of the maturity structure has, in turn, led to considerable concern at both official and unofficial levels about the underlying viability of the euro-currency system.

ANALYTICAL ISSUES

The difficulties in the international economic system that emerged during 1970 and 1971 and the answer to the question, what went wrong?, can perhaps be best understood if we examine the state of thinking at the time with regard to international monetary adjustment. Willms[1] has identified two points of view. The first, which can be associated with Mundell[2] and others, argues that in a world of fixed exchange rates and free capital flows it is not possible for a country to maintain autonomy in the use of domestic monetary policy. For example, consider the case of a country with no balance-of-payments deficit or surplus at the moment but which experiences inflation. A restrictive monetary policy, designed to reduce aggregate demand, will cause interest rates to rise relative to those abroad, thereby inducing an inflow of capital. This in turn produces an over-all surplus in the balance of payments, and hence, as we saw in Chapter 2, an increase in the money supply. To the extent that higher interest rates do temporarily reduce aggregate demand, this will cause imports to fall, and contribute to an even larger balance-of-payments surplus. Thus it would appear that secondary repercussions occur which tend to offset the initial restrictive monetary policy.

The second viewpoint identified by Willms appears to have been the one adopted implicitly by many officials and explicitly by Furth,[3] a former adviser to the Federal Reserve System. He argues that it is 'covered' rather than 'uncovered' interest-rate differentials that generate capital flows. But since the forward exchange rate tends to adjust quickly to the 'uncovered' differentials (as explained in Chapter 3) Furth argues that 'a rise in gross money market rates is not much more likely to set in motion a large inflow of money-market funds than to set in motion an outflow'.

In point of fact both viewpoints neglect the very considerable role played by exchange-rate expectations. Two examples will illustrate what is involved. Suppose that West Germany, along with other European countries, is attempting to follow a restrictive monetary policy whereas the United States is following one of monetary ease. If there is general uncertainty as to future exchange-rate movements or alternatively a widespread view that the Mark will be devalued, then covering in the manner described above makes sense. Not doing so would leave the interest-rate arbitrageur, who had acquired assets in West Germany, open to a reduction in the return on his investment, or perhaps even a capital loss, depending upon the size of any devaluation that might occur. While this action will tend to cause the covered interest-rate differential to narrow, there are a number of factors which might operate so as to prevent its complete elimination. Obviously transactions will determine a minimum spread between interest rates before it becomes profitable to undertake arbitrage. In addition, Branson[4] has estimated that arbitrageurs require a minimum profit over and above transactions costs of 0·18 per cent per annum before they will act. Then demand and supply conditions in the forward market play a role as well. In the above example arbitrageurs will be selling Marks forward. But if there are insufficient persons available to buy forward, then a situation could arise where the dollar price of forward Marks falls by more than is necessary to just offset the interest-rate differential.

This possibility leads us to the second example. Suppose that there is widespread expectation of an upward revaluation of the Mark. To cover these circumstances would mean forgoing any capital gains that might arrive from such a revaluation. Thus, in these circumstances, it is quite likely that the excess supply of forward Marks that occurred in the previous case will not materialise. There will be little or no incentive for the covered interest-rate differential to be eliminated. Indeed, it is likely that this differential may even be widened. Speculators will not only buy the revaluation-prone currency spot, the Mark in our example, but will also seek to buy it forward since this latter action does not involve committing available funds. Foreign traders, and others with previously uncovered net liability positions in dollars, will now wish to cover their positions either by selling dollars spot or by buying forward Marks.

Thus the answer to the question of whether money matters in a world of fixed exchange rates and free capital flows is that *it all depends* – it depends on how speculators, arbitrageurs and foreign traders formulate their expectations. It was perhaps the failure of economists and officials to recognise this crucial element that made it so difficult for U.S. and European economic authorities to come to grips with the implications of the significant international financial interdependence that had been occurring throughout the euro-currency system. Let us now turn to the record.

THE EVENTS OF 1970 AND 1971

By 1970 the excess-demand conditions in the United States stimulated by escalation of the war in South-east Asia were coming to an end. In addition to the restrictive monetary policy followed by the Federal Reserve, as discussed in the previous chapter, Congress had also enacted a 10 per cent Federal income-tax surcharge in 1968. With military expenditures beginning to decline and expectations becoming increasingly pessimistic, the pace of economic activity began to slow down. Unemployment which stood at 3·6 per cent of the labour force at the end of 1969 increased steadily to 6·2 per cent by the end of 1970. In an attempt to moderate such declines, the Federal Reserve actively began to encourage a moderate growth in the U.S. money supply during 1970. Interest rates fell dramatically. In addition, the income-tax surcharge was reduced to 5 per cent in January of that year and eliminated entirely in July.

While stimulating economic activity was an important objective of Federal Reserve policy in 1970, the orderly functioning of financial markets became of increasing concern. As it became clear that the Penn Central Railroad was about to fail, defaulting on large amounts of commercial paper, it was obvious that other corporations which had relied on this technique would find it difficult to refinance their maturing paper. As a result, corporations would place a heavy demand for funds on commercial banks. The Federal Reserve Bank of New York, followed by other branches, gave assurances to their members that funds would be available via the discount window. Thus a policy of ease was also called for to maintain the viability of the U.S. financial system. In addition, and this would have a considerable impact on the euro-currency system, beginning in June 1970 the Regulation Q ceilings on time deposits of $100,000 or more and with maturities of thirty to eighty-nine days were suspended. This was done so as to enable banks to compete more effectively for funds needed to finance their corporate customers. It also considerably reduced the incentive for banks to borrow dollars from their foreign branches.*

While the United States followed a policy of monetary ease during 1970, most European countries, on the other hand, were concerned with stemming the relatively high rates of inflation that they had been experiencing. A particularly vigorous policy was followed in West Germany by the deutsche Bundesbank which raised its discount rate and also the Lombard rate, the rate at which banks may borrow using as collateral securities not covered under the discount facility. However, the combination of this policy together with that of monetary ease in the United States, generated substantial capital inflows into West Germany via the euro-currency system. Not only was there considerable incentive for straight interest-rate arbitrage to occur, but covered differentials moved in West Germany's favour as well. As a result it became advantageous for Germans (and other Europeans) to borrow dollars in the euro-currency system and then sell them on the foreign-exchange market for their own currency. In order to discourage this type of activity, the deutsche Bundesbank imposed progressively higher reserve requirements on banks' foreign liabilities. However, this did not prevent non-bank institutions from borrowing abroad, with the result that German corporations obtained more than 4000 million dollars from the euro-currency system in 1970.

If no other policies had been undertaken, the net result of the conflicting policies followed in the United States and West Germany was to make the application of restrictive monetary policies in Europe increasingly difficult. The inflow of funds via the euro-currency system not only provided German business with a direct, alternative source of funds but also provided their banks with loanable funds that otherwise would not have been available. In addition, the free flow of capital internationally would, in principle, tend to weaken the policy of monetary ease being followed in the United States. As German rates rose above those available in the United States it became less profitable for the foreign branches of U.S. banks to lend funds to their head office. Thus a source of loanable funds to the latter was being bid away.

However, the capital flows that occurred were not simply a result of the divergent trends in monetary policy in Europe and the United

* Subsequently in May 1973, the ceiling was also lifted for deposits maturing in ninety days to more than one year.

States. The Federal Reserve had been openly concerned at the ability of banks with foreign branches to offset the previous restrictive monetary policy through borrowing euro-dollars. As we have already noted, the Federal Reserve modified Regulation Q so as to exempt most certificates of deposit from interest-rate ceilings. This meant that U.S. banks could effectively compete for dollar funds at home. However, initially in 1969 the Federal Reserve sought to 'penalise' bank borrowing abroad through amendments to Regulations D and M. Under the latter a 10 per cent reserve requirement was established on the sum of (1) net borrowings of member banks from their foreign branches, and (2) assets acquired by foreign branches from head offices. This reserve requirement was applicable on the amount by which this sum exceeded the average amount outstanding in the four weeks ending 28 May 1969. This reserve-free base, however, would be reduced if and when actual totals fell below the initial base level. But all member banks with foreign branches were allowed to have a minimum reserve-free base of 3 per cent of deposits. In addition, members of the Federal Reserve System were also subject to a 10 per cent reserve requirement against borrowings from foreign banks to the extent that such borrowings exceeded 4 per cent of a bank's average deposits subject to reserve requirements. Below that only a 3 per cent reserve requirement was applicable. This latter percentage was designed to reduce inequities for banks that did not possess foreign branches. Otherwise all borrowings of euro-dollars from foreign banks would be subject to a 10 per cent reserve requirement. Those banks with branches abroad, however, could benefit from a reserve-free base.

The result of these actions was to increase the effective cost of borrowing by U.S. banks from the euro-dollar system depending upon (1) the channel through which the funds are borrowed, and (2) the level of a bank's previous participation in the system. Although a bank might now pay the normal market euro-dollar rate for funds only a fraction of the proceeds could actually be used for bank loans. Thus to calculate the true or effective euro-dollar rate, it is necessary to divide the actual rate by the proportion of funds that can be loaned out, that is the

$$\text{effective euro-dollar rate} = \frac{\text{market euro-dollar rate}}{1 \cdot 00 - \text{reserve requirement}}.$$

Table 8.1 illustrates the costs involved under the 1969 amendments to Regulations D and M.

The net result of these actions that have been described so far was a dramatic reduction in U.S.-bank borrowing from branches. Fortunately, at the end of 1969 the Federal Reserve began to collect reasonably detailed data on the assets and liabilities of these branches as shown in Table 8.2. Between the end of 1969 and the end of 1974,

TABLE 8.1

Effective cost of euro-dollar borrowing by U.S. banks

	Required reserve ratio	Euro-dollar market rate (percentage)	Effective cost
Member-bank borrowings			
From own foreign branches			
Below base*	0·0	10·25	10·250
Above base	10·0	10·25	11·379
From foreign banks other than own foreign branches			
Demand deposits	10·0	10·25	11·369
Time deposits			
Below base†	3·0	10·25	10·567
Above base	10·0	10·25	11·389
From brokers or dealers	0·0	10·25	‡
Non-member-bank borrowings	0·0	10·25	§

* The base is determined by a bank's daily average borrowing in the four-week period ending 28 May 1969, or any subsequent four-week computation period.
† The base amounts to 4 per cent of a bank's daily average deposits subject to reserve requirements over the computation period.
‡ The effective cost of obtaining euro-dollars through brokers and dealers depends on the commission charged as well as the nature of the bank's relation to the broker and/or dealer. Consequently this rate would vary from transaction to transaction even with the market rate steady at 10·25 per cent.
§ The effective cost would depend on whether the euro-dollars were borrowed directly or through a broker or dealer.

SOURCE: Federal Reserve Bank of Cleveland, 'The Euro-dollar Market', *Economic Review* (Apr 1970) p. 8.

foreign-branch claims on their head offices fell from 13,660 million to 3846 million dollars. As a proportion of total foreign-branch assets this reduction is even more marked. At the end of 1969 such head-office borrowing accounted for 37 per cent of branch assets, falling off to 4 per cent at the end of 1971, a proportion which has been approximately maintained since.

THE EMERGING CRISIS

The Federal Reserve was quick to realise the implications for European monetary policy of its own attempts to reduce bank dependence on the

TABLE 8.2

Assets of foreign branches of U.S. banks

end of year	Total	Claims on United States		Total	Other branches of parent bank	Claims on foreigners		
		Total	Parent bank			Other banks	Official institutions	Non-bank foreigners
1969	36,468	15,380	13,660	20,145	3,524	9,756	537	6,327
1970	47,279	9,686	7,248	36,192	6,881	16,979	695	11,636
1971	59,807	4,753	2,300	53,296	11,210	23,520	1,164	17,401
1972	78,202	4,678	2,113	71,304	11,504	35,773	1,594	22,432
1973	121,866	5,091	1,886	111,974	19,177	56,368	2,693	33,736
1974	151,529	6,280	3,846	138,960	27,536	60,220	4,075	47,129

Liabilities of foreign branches of U.S. banks

end of year	Total	To United States		Total	Other branches of parent bank	To foreigners		
		Total	Parent bank			Other banks	Official institutions	Non-bank foreigners
1969	36,468	2,615	719	32,316	3,534	20,491	1,856	5,942
1970	47,270	2,575	716	42,746	6,372	24,820	4,180	7,374
1971	59,809	3,061	658	54,679	10,743	29,765	5,472	8,699
1972	78,203	3,501	997	72,121	11,121	41,218	8,351	11,432
1973	121,866	5,126	1,158	111,615	18,213	65,625	10,196	17,581
1974	151,529	11,655	5,481	132,943	26,950	65,683	20,133	20,178

SOURCE: *Federal Reserve Bulletin* (1972–5).

euro-currency system, and introduced a number of actions designed to slow down the repayment of funds. First, the marginal reserve requirements which had been imposed in 1969 under Regulations D and M were raised from 10 to 20 per cent. It will be recalled that if U.S. bank liabilities to their foreign branches fell below the May 1969 benchmark, the reserve-free base would also fall. Thus, henceforward, any attempt by banks to reverse the downward trend would mean that they would face a higher marginal reserve requirement and hence a higher effective cost of euro-dollar borrowing. The Federal Reserve hoped that this action would cause the banks to take a 'second look' at drawing down their liabilities too quickly.

However, any effect that this may have had was short-lived, bank repayments being resumed at the beginning of 1971. New initiatives were introduced. In January and February, the Export–Import Bank* offered 1500 million dollars worth of special three-month securities to the foreign branches with the provision that any purchases of these securities could be counted as part of the reserve-free base. Then in April, the U.S. Treasury made a similar offering of special three-month certificates of indebtedness. The net result of these actions was to

FIGURE 8.1   *Liabilities of U.S. banks to foreign branches*

---

* The Export–Import Bank is a U.S. government agency capable of extending and guaranteeing trade credits.

absorb funds which might otherwise have flowed into Europe, thus making the operation of monetary policy there even more difficult (see Figure 8.1). By the end of 1971, however, all such special borrowings had been terminated, and the funds ultimately placed in the euro-currency system.

The sequence of events described above set into motion an apparently irreversible process which not only had fundamental implications for the operation of domestic monetary policy in a world of free international capital flows but also spelled a death-knell to the Bretton Woods adjustable-peg exchange-rate system. As foreigners converted dollars obtained through the euro-currency system into their own currencies, they caused the United States to suffer a deficit on the official settlements basis of $9800 million although the current-account balance registered a surplus of $2100 million (see Table 8.3). Much of this outflow is reflected in the large capital-account surpluses experienced by West Germany, France and other European industrial countries. Initially, it appeared that the deficit would be financed without strain. Dollars accumulated by the United Kingdom and France were used to repay earlier loans from the I.M.F. Other countries were apparently content to add dollars to their portfolio of international reserves. And the widespread use of reciprocal currency agreements by the Federal Reserve made it appear as if the difficulties were viewed in official circles as being purely temporary.

However, such was not to be the case. Throughout the first months of 1971, funds continued to flow out of the United States to Europe. During the period from February to April of 1971, German corporate borrowing abroad amounted to approximately $2500 million, a figure almost equal to total lending to businesses by the German banking system. In view of West Germany's continued strong current-account balance during 1970 and the surplus on capital account, reversing a deficit in 1969, the Mark became the perfect vehicle for speculative activity.

In such an environment, foreign-exchange markets were particularly vulnerable to any hints that there might be any exchange-rate revaluations. The first such even occurred at the beginning of May when it became apparent that West Germany was seriously considering whether to revalue the Mark or to allow it to float upwards. Immediately, intensive speculative pressure was brought to bear on the Mark with the deutsche Bundesbank forced to buy $1000 million on 3 and 4 May and an additional $1000 million in the first forty minutes of trading on 5 May. At this point the Bundesbank ceased to officially support the dollar – a move almost immediately followed by the Netherlands, Switzerland, Belgium and Austria. As a result the currencies of these countries appreciated. However, a major turning point

TABLE 8.3

Balance of payments for selected industrial countries, 1969–73

(*In billions of U.S. dollars*)

		Current-account balance	Capital-account balance*	Over-all balance†
United	1969	0·7	2·0	2·7
States	1970	2·1	−12·9	−9·8
	1971	−1·7	−29·2	−29·8
	1972	−7·1	−4·1	−10·4
	1973	3·3	−8·6	−5·3
United	1969	1·5	−0·3	1·2
Kingdom	1970	2·0	0·7	3·2
	1971	3·0	3·1	6·5
	1972	0·7	−4·0	−3·0
	1973	−2·3	2·5	0·2
West	1969	2·7	−5·7	−3·0
Germany	1970	1·7	4·3	6·3
	1971	2·0	2·2	4·4
	1972	2·8	2·0	5·0
	1973	6·6	2·5	9·2
France	1969	−1·7	0·6	−1·1
	1970	0·1	1·9	2·1
	1971	1·0	2·3	3·4
	1972	1·0	0·6	1·8
	1973	0·5	−2·5	−2·0
Italy	1969	2·6	−3·1	−0·5
	1970	1·3	−0·9	0·5
	1971	2·3	−1·4	1·1
	1972	2·4	−3·2	−0·7
	1973	−1·3	1·1	−0·3
Japan	1969	2·3	−1·5	0·8
	1970	2·2	−1·1	1·2
	1971	6·0	4·3	10·4
	1972	7·0	−4·1	3·0
	1973	0·2	−6·5	−6·3
Canada	1969	−0·7	0·8	0·1
	1970	0·9	0·5	1·6
	1971	0·3	0·5	0·9
	1972	−0·7	0·9	0·3
	1973	−0·5	—	−0·5
Other	1969	0·6	−0·3	0·3
industrial	1970	−0·3	2·3	2·2
countries‡	1971	0·4	2·4	3·0
	1972	3·1	−0·4	3·0
	1973	3·7	−0·7	3·0

* This balance is computed residually, as the difference between the over-all balance (less S.D.R. allocations) and the current-account balance; it includes official transfers and net errors and omissions, as well as recorded capital movements.
† Over-all balances are measured by changes in official gold holdings, in S.D.R.s, in reserve positions in the Fund, in foreign-exchange assets, in use of Fund credit, and, where data are available, in liabilities to foreign authorities, including those arising from 'swap' transactions.
‡ Austria, Belgium–Luxembourg, Denmark, the Netherlands, Norway and Switzerland.

SOURCE: International Monetary Fund, *Annual Reports*, data reported to the International Monetary Fund staff estimates.

occurred on 6 August when there were again massive flows from the dollar. In response President Nixon announced a 10 per cent temporary surcharge on dutiable imports and a temporary suspension of convertibility of the dollar into gold. Foreign-exchange markets were closed while the U.S. and European governments attempted to work out a joint policy response. This failed, with the result that exchange rates were allowed to seek their own levels under a controlled float. On this same day, the Swiss central bank imposed a 100 per cent reserve requirement against increases in commercial banks' increases in net foreign liabilities.

These events effectively meant the end of the Bretton Woods system. However, without any real alternative framework, there was growing anxiety in all countries that trade restrictions and exchange controls, which had been greatly liberalised since the Second World War, might return. Recognising the growing threat to international trade and payments, the Group of Ten countries agreed on 18 December 1971 to a change in the official price of gold from $35 an ounce to $38 an ounce and to realign exchange rates according to the schema shown in Table 8.4.

TABLE 8.4

Currency	Percentage appreciation of parity against U.S. dollar
Belgian franc	11·57
U.K. pound	8·57
French franc	8·57
German mark	13·58
Italian lire	7·48
Japanese yen	16·88
Netherlands guilder	11·57
Swedish krona	7·49
Swiss franc	6·36

In addition, the band around these new parities was widened from 1 per cent either side to 2·25 per cent either side of parity. In subsequent months any speculative moves were firmly met through intervention and the use of reciprocal currency agreements. Further, the central banks of both the United States and Europe undertook measures to narrow the interest-rate differentials that had originally been the source of difficulty.

The events of 1970 and 1971 made it clear that the exercise of domestic monetary policy in an open international economy was bound to be fraught with difficulties. Willms[5] calculated that between 1958 and 1970 the German monetary authorities had neutralised approximately 86 per cent of inflows from abroad. However, as Schlesinger and

E

Bockelmann have pointed out,[6] Willms's analysis failed to take into account the different circumstances holding during the latter part of the period. While a policy of neutralisation might work some of the time, it could not possibly work all of the time, a conclusion borne out in Table 8.5. Whereas external sources had indeed contributed to the

TABLE 8.5

The main sources of change in the money stock

(In billions of deutsche Marks)

		53-7	57-61	61-5	65-9	67-71
(1)	Increase in money stock	12·2	21·3	19·9	20·9	33·7
(2)	Money creation from external transactions (increase in net external claims)	13·5	10·7	5·8	15·8	34·6
(3)	Money creation from domestic sources (credit expansion less monetary capital formation, increase in quasi-money stock, change in public authorities' central-bank balances, other influences) ie (1) less (2)	−1·3	10·6	14·1	5·1	−0·9
(4)	Ratio of money creation from external transactions (2) to total increase in money stock (1) (in per cent)	110·6	50·1	29·1	75·7	102·6

SOURCE: H. Schlesinger and H. Bockelmann, 'Monetary Policy in the Federal Republic of Germany', in *Monetary Policy in Twelve Industrial Countries*, ed. K. Holbik (Federal Reserve Bank of Boston, 1973) p. 207.

growth of the German money stock between 1957 and 1969, it was not the only source. However, in the period 1967 to 1971, external sources accounted for virtually the entire growth in the money stock.

THE DECLINE AND FALL OF THE BRETTON WOODS SYSTEM

Underlying the Bretton Woods system was an explicit belief that the free international flow of goods, services and investment funds was compatible with a regime of exchange rates which could be held fixed for prolonged periods of time. The events leading up to the Smithsonian Agreement had significantly eroded this position. The free flow of capital not only made it difficult to preserve stable exchange markets; it also made impossible the operation of monetary policy designed to achieve domestic objectives. Initially it had appeared as if the currency realignment might restore stability to the international monetary system. Such hopes, however, were effectively dashed in June 1972 when the United Kingdom suspended its participation in the Smithsonian Agreement and allowed the pound to float.

During the first months of 1972 the United Kingdom had experienced a favourable balance-of-payments position with the result that it had decided to join with the six members of the European Economic Community to maintain a band of 2·25 per cent either side of the Smithsonian parities. As part of this policy the parties agreed to support their exchange rates within the band only with their partners' currencies. However, if the ceiling or floor of the band was reached, then dollar reserves could be used. Thus in June when the pound came under considerable selling pressure, the Bank of England and its European partners co-operated to maintain the pound within the agreed band. However, in the process this intervention also dragged down the values of the stronger continental currencies as they attempted to maintain their value relative to the weaker pound.

Initially the euro-currency system had little impact on the emerging crisis, but when it became clear that exchange rates might again be realigned, there was a rush to borrow dollars to purchase strong continental currencies. Following the U.K. decision to float, the foreign-exchange and international money markets took on some semblance of 'normalcy'. Many European countries, particularly West Germany and Switzerland, had imposed stringent capital controls, and with the dollar strong felt that they could impose more restrictive monetary policies in order to dampen down inflation. However, this action generated a large outflow of funds from the United States and a renewed crisis. And again the euro-currency system played a significant role. Traders and investors who had held dollars in the United States or in the euro-currency system now attempted to cover their positions either by liquidating these dollars or by selling them forward. European banks which had purchased the dollars forward in turn sought to even out their positions by borrowing euro-dollars and then selling the proceeds spot for stronger currencies. As a result of the intense pressure, the United States devalued the dollar in February 1973, with this action followed by an E.E.C. decision in March to jointly float their currencies. There was thus a complete abandonment of the Smithsonian Agreement.

With this as background, let us now examine in some detail the nature of the two major policy responses over this period – (a) the widespread use of capital controls, and (b) greater exchange-rate flexibility.

(a) The imposition of capital controls

Prior to the currency realignment of 1971, most European countries had, at one time or another, imposed capital controls either to increase the effectiveness of domestic monetary policies or to hinder potentially destabilising speculative capital flight. It is true that the United Kingdom has generally operated a very comprehensive and stringent system of exchange controls, with the result that their citizens cannot generally assume foreign-currency positions. However, for most countries, resort to capital controls prior to 1972 had mainly been a temporary expedient. But now their use escalated. The measures took a variety of forms, many establishing conditions under which non-residents could acquire domestic-currency assets. However, as we shall see, several particularly severe restrictions had implications for euro-currency activity.

In general, the capital controls utilised can be divided up into the following categories:

(1) Restrictions on commercial banks' external positions. These would include limits on the expansion of credit by banks, which tends to reduce the incentive for them to incur foreign liabilities. In addition the authorities have imposed limits on net asset–liability positions of banks.

(2) The prohibition of interest payments on deposits placed by non-residents.

(3) Higher reserve requirements against bank liabilities to foreigners than against liabilities to a country's own residents.

(4) Controls designed to restrict foreign borrowing by the non-banking sector.

(5) The use of multiple exchange rates: one, usually constant, for commercial transactions; the other, variable, for financial transactions.

These and other policy measures have been documented by Mills[7] for the 1960s. Analysis of more recent controls is given elsewhere.[8] However, by far the best discussion, both in terms of general international trends and individual country positions, is presented by the I.M.F. in their comprehensive annual reports, *Exchange Restrictions*. From our viewpoint it will be sufficient to examine some of the controls that had a direct impact on the euro-currency system.

One of the most significant was the *Bardepot* imposed by the German Ministry of Economics and Finance. Under this scheme German residents, including banks, may be required to hold with the Bundesbank non-interest-bearing cash deposits denominated in deutsche Marks and amounting to at least 50 per cent of certain categories of borrowing from foreigners. On March 1 1972 a rate of 40 per cent was set retroactive to 1 January. This had the immediate effect of curbing the widespread practice whereby German corporations borrowed eurodollars, which they then converted into Marks. In July 1972 the deposit rate was raised to 50 per cent and, subsequently in February 1973, the *Bardepot* law was amended so as to allow a 100 per cent maximum rate. However, this possibility has not been exercised and, in fact, as of 1 February 1974, the rate was reduced to 20 per cent.

Controls were also brought to bear on the activities of German commercial banks. First, they were prohibited from paying interest on deutsche Mark and euro-currency deposits held by non-residents. In addition, in June 1971 the Bundesbank imposed a 30 per cent reserve requirement against commercial banks' foreign liabilities, a rate twice as high as the one for domestic liabilities. Further, an *additional* 30 per cent reserve requirement on *increases* in liabilities to non-residents had been in force since December 1970 and was maintained. During 1972 these requirements were further tightened in a series of moves that effectively meant that 90–100 per cent of any *new* non-resident liabilities had to be held as reserves with the Bundesbank. Depending on the maturity date of the deposit, the *minimum* reserve requirement against external liabilities was set in a range of 30 to 40 per cent.

A second country imposing increasingly restrictive controls affecting the euro-currency system was Switzerland. In general, Swiss banks were prohibited from paying interest on deposits of non-residents denominated in Swiss francs. Euro-currency deposits were excluded. However, on 16 August 1971 a gentleman's agreement between the Swiss National Bank and the Swiss Bankers' Association came into effect. This arrangement provided that the National Bank could impose a minimum reserve requirement of up to 100 per cent against any increase in commercial banks' liabilities, denominated in both Swiss francs and foreign currencies, and held by non-residents. Any simultaneous increase in banks' assets held abroad could be used to count against these liabilities for the purpose of calculating the amount subject to the requirement. Immediately the National Bank imposed a 100 per cent requirement against new deposits placed by non-residents in Swiss francs after 31 July. In July 1972, a Federal Ordinance was instituted which required that commercial banks should have covered foreign positions at the close of business each day. This would have the dual effect of damping down speculation and preventing banks from taking dollar liabilities and converting them to Swiss francs. In October, the National Bank imposed an 80 per cent reserve requirement against gross liabilities in foreign currencies, where any increase in these liabilities was not offset by a corresponding increase in foreign assets. The net result of this action was to make the utilisation of funds obtained via euro-currency deposits highly costly.

In March 1973 a new set of reserve requirements was introduced which differentiated between euro-currency deposits and deposits denominated in Swiss francs. In addition reserve ratios were set against the growth in foreign liabilities as well as the level. These are shown in Table 8.6.

(b) Exchange-rate flexibility*

No international monetary system can be perfect. Costs of one sort or

* For a full discussion of the events surrounding the use of floating exchange rates over this period, see Katz on 'managed floating'.[9]

TABLE 8.6

	Minimum reserve ratios on growth of foreign liabilities	Reserve ratios on level of foreign liabilities	
	Swiss francs or foreign currencies	*Swiss francs*	*Foreign currencies*
Demand or time deposits at banks	56	3	1·5
Time deposits at non-banks	42	2	1
Savings deposits	7	—	—

another are bound to be involved, with the result that one 'system' may be relevant for one point in time, whereas another may be more appropriate for another set of circumstances. It is clear that the Bretton Woods system was what was required to remove uncertainty and restore confidence following (*a*) the Second World War, which had disrupted the international economy, and (*b*) prior to that, a period of massive depression, trade restrictions and economic warfare. Undoubtedly fixed exchange rates provided the necessary environment in which increased international trade, recovery and hence sustained economic growth could occur. However, in the 1960s, following the restoration of full exchange convertibility, it became clear to many that the system was not viable. Because changes in par values are discretionary and their timing and magnitude are extremely difficult for officials to determine, exchange rates tended to be altered only as a last resort under the Bretton Woods system.

This meant that a country could build up a long history of deficits or surpluses with the result that the probability of an exchange-rate adjustment occurring had to increase with time. Speculators could move funds into strong currencies with little risk that the exchange rate would move in a direction counter to their expectations. And any rumour of a readjustment could potentially cause such an outflow of capital and loss of reserves for the country whose currency was under attack that an exchange-rate change became inevitable. Speculators' expectations became self-fulfilling.

Because decisions to alter the exchange rate typically are postponed, when the adjustment does occur it tends to be relatively large in magnitude, being concentrated within a short period of time on the importing and exporting sectors of the initiating country and its trading partners. On the other hand, failure to undertake such adjustments may be equally costly. If a country's payments deficit is due to costs and prices rising faster at home than abroad, domestic export- and import-competing industries will find business dwindling.

In addition, as we have emphasised in this and the previous chapter, an international monetary system based on fixed exchange rates and encouraging the free flow of capital renders the use of monetary policy ineffective. However, under a system of flexible rates this is no longer the case. To illustrate this, let us return to our earlier example where it was assumed that West Germany was experiencing inflation and the Bundesbank sought to restrain economic activity by following a restrictive monetary policy. As interest rates rise, investors will find, as before, German assets relatively attractive, and the increased demand for Marks will cause it to appreciate relative to other currencies. As this occurs, West Germany's exportables tend to become more expensive abroad while imports become cheaper relative to domestically produced goods. Demand for home-produced goods falls – the objective of the restrictive monetary policy. Because the exchange rate is free to adjust to market conditions, there are no balance-of-payments deficits or surpluses and hence no offsetting monetary effect.

As with the adjustable-peg system, the formation of expectations by speculators and traders is bound to play a significant role under a flexible rate system. Friedman[10] has taken the extreme position that such operators are virtually omniscient about the nature of any future exchange-rate movements. For example, suppose that the Mark/dollar exchange rate has *temporarily* fallen below its long-run equilibrium level. In this case, so Friedman would argue, speculators would become net purchasers of dollars, and in the process would bid up the exchange rate thereby returning it to its long-run equilibrium. Alternatively, suppose that the actual Mark/dollar rate is higher than that which market forces will dictate in the future. Again, it is argued that operators, being 'intelligent', will foresee this situation and become net purchasers of Marks. This activity also moves the exchange rate in the 'correct' direction.

However, there is no particular reason why speculators and traders should be so omniscient. There may be situations where they believe that the rate should fall when underlying real factors call for an increase. In the long run the error may be recognised, but in the short run the response to a false signal could set up undesirable exchange-rate fluctuations. If one believes that the probability is high of such errors unduly influencing markets, then the central banks can always intervene to control the direction and speed of movement of rates. Indeed this is the current situation. The United Kingdom and the other countries which have floating rates do not allow them to move perfectly freely but rather attempt to smooth out any fluctuations which the authorities believe to be undesirable. Under such a system each country is still required to hold reserves but the magnitude of changes in this variable will not be as great as under a perfectly fixed rate system, since exchange-rate movements should eliminate, at least partly, any excess supply of or demand for foreign exchange.

In theory the emergence of a floating exchange-rate system should have considerable implications for the euro-currency system. The existence of greater risk of capital losses in the short term arising from adverse exchange-rate movements should make operators adverse to assuming as large foreign-exchange positions as they would under a system of fixed rates. Thus one might argue that foreign traders, banks, perhaps even central banks, should be motivated to reduce their working balances denominated in foreign currencies, particularly with respect to the major vehicle of the system, the dollar, which has been depreciating over this period. It is true that euro-bank liabilities in stronger currencies, particularly the deutsche Mark and Swiss franc, have increased over this period. But, on the other hand, the euro-dollar component of the system does not appear to have been adversely affected.

There are several reasons for this. First, to the extent that the benefits from holding euro-currency or other foreign assets outweigh potential or actual losses from exchange-rate variations, there is still an incentive to hold funds in this form. This is likely to be the case when actual exchange-rate movements are relatively small over short periods of time. Second, to the extent that covering facilities are available, for example via the forward market, then such operations may be used to offset any potential losses from holding euro-dollar or other currency deposits. Third, to the extent that exchange rates do vary over time, the euro-currency system may provide attractive instruments for speculation. For example, if it is expected that a particular currency is going to appreciate, then a long euro-currency position would be called for. On the other hand, if a depreciation was expected, then a short position in that currency would be the course of action. Thus it would appear that even under a floating exchange-rate system the transactions, precautionary and speculative motives for holding euro-currency deposits would still be operative.

PETRO-CURRENCY RECYCLING

The second important set of circumstances affecting the euro-currency system during the early 1970s involved the rapid increases in the prices of primary products, not only oil but a whole range of basic commodities. These increases, excluding oil, are dramatised in Figure 8.2.[11] The result has been an improved balance-of-payments position for both the developed and developing countries producing and exporting these products, and for many an actual increase in their stock of international reserves. As a result the monetary authorities of those benefiting have

TABLE 8.7

Identified official holdings of euro-currencies, end of years, 1969–73

(*In billions of dollars*)

	1969	1970	1971*	1972	1973†
Identified official euro-currency holdings‡					
Euro-dollars					
Industrial countries	2·2	5·1	3·7	6·2	6·2
Primary-producing countries					
More-developed areas	0·5	1·4	2·1	3·1	3·6
Less-developed areas	2·0	3·8	5·8	9·4	11·6
Western hemisphere	0·6	1·2	1·6	3·7	4·5
Middle East	0·4	0·6	1·2	2·1	2·9
Asia	0·5	1·0	1·1	2·0	3·0
Africa	0·5	1·1	1·7	1·8	1·2
Total, primary-producing countries	2·5	5·2	7·8	12·6	15·2
of which, major oil producers	0·8	1·5	3·0	4·2	5·8
Grand total	4·7	10·3	11·5	18·9	21·5
Other euro-currencies	—	—	1·8	3·9	6·4

* Includes the change in the level of holdings owing to the effect of the realignment in December.
† Includes the change in the level of holdings owing to the effect of U.S. dollar devaluation in February.
‡ That is, on central monetary institutions other than those in the United States, the United Kingdom, France or West Germany.

SOURCE: International Monetary Fund, *Annual Report, 1974* (Washington, D.C.) p. 35.

sought to increase their return by placing part of their reserves in the euro-currency system. As is shown in Table 8.7, in 1969 placements by industrial countries accounted for almost one-half of *official* euro-currency holdings. As noted previously in this chapter, the monetary authorities of many in this group agreed to restrict the growth of such deposits largely for reasons of domestic monetary policy. But by the end

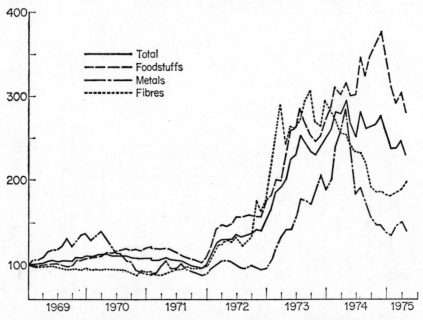

FIGURE 8.2   *World-market commodity prices:* The Economist *indicator (monthly – dollar – indexes: end of 1968 = 100)*

of 1973 total official placements had increased to four times the figure for 1969. Of the $17·8 billion value of these placements, two-thirds are held by primary-producing countries with $4·0 billion held by the major oil producers. While such deposits are not the only form in which the so-called petro-dollar (or perhaps better petro-currency funds) exists they do account for a significant proportion as can be seen from Table 8.8. However, this development represents more than simply another source of funds to the system; there are a number of additional, important implications.

(1) The increase in raw-material prices, particularly that of oil, has not only brought balance-of-payments surpluses to many primary producers, it has also caused many industrial countries to suffer large payments deficits. This situation has led the latter group to seek funds via the euro-currency system to enable them to sustain this imbalance. For

example, the United Kingdom, France and Italy during the first half of 1974 borrowed in excess of $8 billion through government agencies or public-sector institutions.* In addition, several governments also encouraged private-sector enterprises to participate in the system. Again during the first half of 1974, Japanese banks borrowed about $6 billion from the euro-currency system and French private non-banks borrowed $3 million of foreign-currency funds from French banks and from banks domiciled abroad.

TABLE 8·8

Estimated deployment of oil exporters' surplus, 1974

(*billions of dollars*)

United Kingdom		United States	
British government stocks	0·9	Government and agency securities	6·0
Treasury bills	2·7	Bank deposits	4·0
Sterling deposits	1·7	Other*	1·0
Other sterling investments*	0·7		
Foreign-currency deposits	13·8	Total	11·0
Other foreign-currency borrowing	1·2		
		Other countries	
		Foreign-currency deposits	9·0
Total	21·0	Special bilateral facilities and investments*†	11·6
		Total	20·6
		International organisations	3·6

* Includes holdings of equities and property.
† Includes loans to developing countries.

SOURCE: Bank of England, *Quarterly Bulletin* (Mar 1975).

(2) As a result of the changed balance-of-payments situation resulting from the primary price increases, many countries eased or abolished restrictions affecting the euro-currency system. In January 1974 West Germany reduced the minimum reserve requirements against external liabilities by 5 per cent and the 60 per cent marginal reserve requirement on foreign liabilities was abolished. Then in October these minimum requirements were lowered by a further 8 per cent to stand at 32 per cent for sight deposits and to 23 per cent for savings deposits. In

* It will be recalled from our definitions in Chapter 2 that such borrowing would be a credit entry in these countries' balance-of-payments accounts.

addition to other changes in the regulations governing international capital movements, the *Bardepot* scheme, restricting borrowing abroad by German non-bank corporations, was suspended. These actions were taken to stimulate foreign borrowing in anticipation that a deficit on the oil account could adversely affect the deutsche Mark.

Further, in anticipation that the oil-surplus countries would be depositing considerable funds in the United States, that country liberalised restraints on foreign lending by eliminating in January 1974 its interest-equalisation tax, its controls on direct foreign investments by U.S. residents and its voluntary restraints on foreign lending by U.S. financial institutions. As the Bank for International Settlements has indicated in its 1975 *Report*,[12] the implications of these actions for the euro-currency system are difficult to assess. As we noted earlier, the imposition of these controls provided a significant impetus to the further growth of the system. Conversely, one would expect that their removal could possibly lead to a contraction. In any case, the rate of growth of gross euro-currency liabilities slowed down somewhat during 1974, although liabilities to non-banks continued to expand at a vigorous pace. On the other hand, the Bank has argued that if the United States should attract an overly large share of the oil surpluses, it could indeed rechannel these into the euro-currency system, thus stimulating its further growth. To a certain extent this did occur. Assets, mainly denominated in dollars, of U.S. banks to their foreign branches rose considerably from $1158 million at the end of 1973 to $5481 million at the end of 1974. Total claims on foreign banks by U.S. banks nearly doubled over this same period from $4555 million to $7430 million.

(3) A further implication of the large inflow of funds into the euro-currency system was a modification in the maturity structure of liabilities and assets. What has occurred is that the oil-producing and other surplus countries placing funds in the system have preferred to hold predominantly short-term instruments. This is quite understandable since it is presumably the goal of many of these countries to ultimately place their assets in longer-run investment projects. On the other hand, the borrowing governments and public agencies of deficit countries wanted to acquire funds for relatively longer periods of time. In addition the apparent glut of funds flowing into the system induced euro-banks to seek new outlets, including agencies in developing countries who wished to borrow for relatively long periods and other, perhaps risky, ventures. This situation is summarised in Table 8.9 where there are presented liability–asset ratios of U.K. banks according to category of lender/borrower and maturity for July 1969 and November 1974. It will be noted first that the ratio of assets to liabilities of U.K. banks *vis-à-vis* one another are approximately one and have remained unchanged. The category 'Other U.K. residents' is relatively unimportant

and can be neglected. On the other hand, the maturity structure of U.K. banks *vis-à-vis* foreign banks has changed. In 1969, short-term assets (up to three months) were greater than short-term liabilities whereas the reverse was true for instruments maturing in a year or longer. However, by November 1974, U.K. banks had become net short-term borrowers from foreign banks and net long-term lenders to them. Such

TABLE 8.9

Maturity analysis of liabilities and assets
of U.K. banks in foreign currencies

	Liability–asset ratios			
Maturity	U.K. inter-bank	Other U.K. residents	Banks abroad	Other non-residents
November 1974				
Up to 3 months	0·97	1·16	1·34	1·28
3 months to 1 year	1·02	0·30	1·37	0·62
1 year and longer	0·98	<0·01	0·93	0·10
Over-all position	0·98	0·42	1·30	0·62
July 1969				
Up to 3 months	1·01	2·18	0·86	1·93
3 months to 1 year	0·96	0·41	1·10	1·78
1 year and longer	0·98	<0·01	1·26	0·19
Over-all position	1·00	0·90	0·91	1·33

SOURCE: Bank of England, *Quarterly Bulletin* (various dates).

a situation has always characterised the position with respect to non-residents. However, it significantly deteriorated between the two periods. Whereas in 1969 liabilities and assets of one year or more stood at £143 million and £765 million, respectively, the same categories in November 1974 were £634 million and £6469 million.

While these available figures refer only to the operations of U.K. euro-banks, they generally reflect the maturity structure of the euro-currency system as a whole. It is therefore quite easy to appreciate the apprehension that developed over the failure of the Bankhaus Herstatt of Germany in June 1974 and, simultaneously, the continuing problems of the Franklin National Bank in New York – which became, ultimately, insolvent in October 1974. With regard to Herstatt, a large proportion of its losses were the result of taking highly risky and aggressive foreign-exchange positions. And when it ceased operating, it left other banks, both German and foreign, with virtually worthless claims against it. Other major banks were affected as well. In September 1974 *The Economist* estimated that foreign-exchange losses of several major banks were as is shown in Table 8.10. The result was that it became increasingly difficult for relatively small banks to raise needed funds either via the euro-currency system or through other channels.

Offsetting this deterioration of confidence throughout the international banking community were several steps taken by central banks. In the wake of the Herstatt affair, the deutsche Bundesbank expanded

TABLE 8.10

Herstatt	£65 million
Union Bank of Switzerland	£65 million
Westdeutsche Landesbank	£45 million
Lloyds Bank	£33 million
Franklin National	£20 million

SOURCE: *The Economist* (7 Sep 1974) p. 94.

its credit facilities to German banks although on a selective basis. Prior to the failure of the Franklin National Bank, the Federal Reserve Bank of New York, in consultation with the Board of Governors and the U.S. Treasury, acquired the foreign-exchange commitments of this bank. This action thereby headed off any potential, speculative run on the dollar. In addition, the Federal Reserve indicated that it would be willing to support any soundly managed member bank should it fall victim to liquidity problems arising from large-scale withdrawals of petro-dollars.

A further significant event occurred on 10 September 1974 when the Bank for International Settlements announced that the central banks of the countries comprising the Group of Ten were able and willing to act as lenders of last resort should banks operating in the euro-currency system experience liquidity problems. For purposes of this agreement, responsibility for banks' foreign branches would rest with the central bank of the country in which the branch, not the head office, was domiciled. In addition, the Bank of England obtained firm commitments from major U.K. banks that they had a moral commitment to support banks operating in the euro-currency system should the need arise.

While the above formula falls short of creating an international central bank which can act as lender of last resort to euro-banks in much the same way as national central banks act towards domestic commercial banks, it does represent a significant step forward. Not only do each of the Group of Ten hold large stocks of international reserves, they have also negotiated reciprocal currency arrangements which could be drawn on should the need arise. Indeed, as we saw in the previous chapter, they and the B.I.S. have already developed a considerable expertise in ironing out seasonal imbalances as well as speculative runs affecting the system.

FURTHER READING

Bank for International Settlements, *Annual Report* (1974–5).

W. Branson, 'The Minimum Covered Interest Differential Needed for International Arbitrage Activity', *Journal of Political Economy* (Nov–Dec 1969).

M. Friedman, 'The Case for Flexible Exchange Rates', in his *Essays in Positive Economics* (Chicago University Press, 1953).

J. H. Furth, 'International Monetary Reform and the "Crawling Peg:" Comment', *Review of the Federal Reserve Bank of St Louis* (July 1969).

S. I. Katz, ' "Managed Floating" as an Interim International Exchange Rate Regime, 1973–1975', *Bulletin of the Schools of Business of New York University*, no. 3 (1975).

R. M. Mills, 'The Regulation of Short-Term Capital Movements: Western European Techniques in the 1960's, *Staff Economic Studies*, no. 46, Board of Governors of the Federal Reserve System, Washington, D.C. (1968).

R. Mundell, *International Economics* (New York: Macmillan, 1968).

Organization for Economic Co-operation and Development, 'Controls on Capital Flows', *Economic Outlook* (Dec 1972).

H. Schlesinger and H. Bockelmann, 'Monetary Policy in the Federal Republic of Germany', in *Monetary Policy in Twelve Industrial Countries*, ed. K. Holbik (Federal Reserve Bank of Boston, 1973).

M. Willms, 'Controlling Money in an Open Economy: The German Case', *Review of the Federal Reserve Bank of St Louis* (Apr 1971).

9

A Postscript: Some Thoughts on International Economic Interdependence

The central problem of international economic co-operation is how to take advantage of the benefits inherent in economic interdependence while at the same time maintaining autonomy in the pursuit of legitimate economic objectives.* This has been the dilemma posed by the euro-currency system. Reconsider first the benefits which we discussed in Chapters 3 and 4. It is true that gains would occur to deficit and surplus economic units from international trade in financial items even if the euro-currency system did not exist. However, for technical and legal reasons and because the system enjoys certain economies of scale, it is able to provide to its customers more attractive services, a wider range of maturities and highly competitive borrowing and lending rates than are available in alternative financial markets. As a result, operators in the system find themselves in a preferred portfolio position capable of increasing both their current consumption and savings levels. The benefits are thus analogous to those associated with the well-known gains from international commodity trade.

The cost of greater international interdependence is the loss of *national autonomy*, the ability to conceive and to actually carry out policy objectives. As Cooper has pointed out, there are two aspects to this problem. First, in a world of uncertainty there is no reason why prices, interest rates and expenditure will always adjust so that a country's balance-of-payments deficits or surpluses will be zero. Thus each country must maintain international reserves which it must draw upon in the case of deficit, or accumulate in the case of surplus, if the exchange rate is to be held constant. In the former instance the authorities must realise that unless they can borrow sufficient funds abroad, their stock of reserves is limited. As a result they must often turn to other measures, expenditure-switching or expenditure-changing policies which work to eliminate any imbalance. But such measures may have undesirable implications on the level of employment, output and prices not only at home but also abroad. While it is true that the existence of the euro-currency system cannot be viewed as the only or the main cause of the balance-of-payments difficulties of the late 1960s and early 1970s, it must be viewed as a contributor. By acting as a significant staging area for speculative activities, particularly against the dollar, it helped to

* For an excellent discussion of the issues involved, see Cooper's *The Economics of Interdependence*.[1]

bring to an end the Bretton Woods system and thus to affect the environment in which each and every member of the I.M.F. would formulate and carry out domestic and international economic policies.

A second way in which a country may lose national autonomy arises from the effect that international interdependence has on its ability to regulate business and finance. With respect to the euro-currency system there are two main aspects, one basically monetary, the other arising from the nature of financial intermediation.

MONETARY CONSIDERATIONS

As we have shown in the previous two chapters, the effective use of monetary policy under a regime of fixed exchange rates and with unrestricted capital movements is very difficult to achieve. For example, if we start from a position of full equilibrium, any attempt by the authorities to follow a restrictive policy leading to higher interest rates will lead to a surplus on capital account. And to the extent that there is a reduction in expenditure in general, and in imports in particular, there will also be a surplus on current account. This, in turn, means that the country under consideration will find that its cash balances are increasing, thereby offsetting the aims of the original restrictive policy.

All this, of course, could occur in the absence of the euro-currency system. The question is whether the speed of response of capital movements would be as quick. Consider the following argument. Suppose that the 'country' trying to follow the restrictive monetary policy in the above example is really the state of California. *Ceteris paribus*, a higher return on the Californian securities does not necessarily mean that investors on the East coast of the United States will immediately sell securities issued locally in order to buy ones in California. For one thing, investors in the East will not have direct access to the information that Californians do. And different legal regulations may govern financial transactions in the two areas. For these reasons investors in the East may respond only slowly and warily to the higher return in California. If this is the case, then, at least in the short run, the restrictive monetary policy may have some effectiveness. However, as Ingram has pointed out,[2] there does exist a substantial pool of securities which are nationally acceptable, for example U.S. Treasury bills. Thus, in the above example, Californians will sell their Treasury bills in order to buy the higher-yielding local securities. This, in turn, will lead to higher-yielding bills and will induce Easterners to sell their own local securities for the Treasury bills. Instead of there being a direct flow of funds between the two regions, there is an indirect flow which is likely to be larger and faster depending on just how widely acceptable are the national securities.

A completely analogous situation exists within the euro-currency system. Its existence not only increases the potential for flows of funds *between* the United States and Europe, it also increases the potential for flows *within* Europe. For example, suppose that in the absence of any restrictions West Germany attempts to follow a restrictive monetary policy. This provides an incentive for those holding euro-dollar assets to sell them in favour of German assets. Similarly, it now becomes relatively attractive for Germans to borrow in the system rather than at home. These actions have the effect of bidding up euro-dollar yields with the result that funds will in turn be drawn from other national money markets. In other words, euro-currency assets are in a position to perform the same function as U.S. Treasury bills do in the United States. But at the same time that the national money markets are more closely linked, national monetary authorities find themselves less able to achieve domestic objectives.

PROBLEMS OF INTERMEDIATION

A *potential* obstacle to the formulation and execution of national policies arises from the role of euro-banks as financial intermediaries. As we emphasised in Chapter 4 and again in Chapter 8, euro-banks transmute liabilities denominated in one currency (usually dollars) into assets possessing different properties: they may be of longer maturity, of a higher degree of riskiness, and provided that there are no legal restrictions they may be denominated in a different currency than the original deposit. While this transmutation enables euro-banks to meet the desires of their customers on the one hand, and to make profits for its own account, it also introduces the potential for instability not only for the euro-currency system itself but also for the entire international-payments system.

Suppose that interest rates are more attractive for alternative financial instruments than for euro-currency deposits. If this situation should continue there will be a large withdrawal of funds from the system. In order to meet their customers' requirements, euro-banks must attempt to sell some assets. However, if they are particularly risky and of long maturity, then they may find that their assets are not easily marketable. If this is the case they may be forced into bankruptcy with the result that there will be widespread loss of confidence in the system. Further, investors may attempt to reduce their foreign-currency positions, particularly those held in the system, until confidence is restored. And this, in turn, can cause payments problems for those countries whose currencies are affected. As a result the authorities may be forced to impose restrictions or to undertake policies which affect relative prices and expenditure levels and which otherwise would not have been contemplated.

If a similar situation were to arise within a domestic banking system, its impact would be considerably reduced. The central bank would act as a lender of last resort, thereby ensuring stability in domestic money markets. If bankruptcies should occur many depositors would be protected by officially sponsored insurance schemes. However, there is no similar arrangement for the euro-currency system. Since it transcends national boundaries, it must rely on the goodwill of the authorities involved to step in and ensure the stability of international financial and foreign-exchange markets. There is no international central bank with powers to act in a manner similar to that of a domestic central bank, although as we noted in the previous chapter the major central banks agreed in 1974 to assume some of these responsibilities.

In many respects, then, the picture that we have been painting throughout this volume is that of a system balancing on a knife-edge. On the one hand, there are the benefits which accrue from its activities as a financial intermediary. On the other hand, it acts as a vehicle for its own destruction by making it difficult for the authorities to carry out domestic monetary policies and to maintain the stability of the international-payments system. As we have seen in Chapters 7 and 8, restrictions have been increasingly placed on international capital flows including those passing through the euro-currency system.

FURTHER READING

R. N. Cooper, *The Economics of Interdependence* (New York: McGraw-Hill, 1968).
J. C. Ingram, 'A Proposal for Financial Integration in the Atlantic Community', in *Factors Affecting the United States Balance of Payments*, Joint Economic Committee of the Congress of the United States (Washington, D.C., 1962).

References

CHAPTER ONE

1. G. McKenzie, 'International Monetary Reform and the "Crawling Peg" ', *Review of the Federal Reserve Bank of St Louis* (Feb 1969), reprinted in *Monetary Economics*, ed. J. Prager (New York: Random House, 1971) pp. 408–16; and 'Reply', *Review of the Federal Reserve Bank of St Louis* (July 1969) pp. 26–31.

2. J. H. Furth, 'International Monetary Reform and the "Crawling Peg" – Comment', *Review of the Federal Reserve Bank of St Louis* (July 1969) pp. 21–5.

3. J. Prager, *Monetary Economics* (New York: Random House, 1971) p. 408.

4. J. G. Gurley and E. S. Shaw, *Money in a Theory of Finance* (Washington, D.C.: The Brookings Institution, 1960).

5. J. Tobin, 'Commercial Banks as Creators of "Money" ', in *Banking and Monetary Studies*, ed. D. Carson (Homewood, Ill.: Irwin, 1963) pp. 408–19.

6. B. J. Moore, *An Introduction to the Theory of Finance* (New York: The Free Press, 1968).

7. P. Davidson, *Money and the Real World* (London: Macmillan, 1972).

8. G. Bell, *The Eurodollar Market and the International Financial System* (London: Macmillan, 1973).

9. P. Einzig, *The Eurobond Market* (London: Macmillan, 1969); and *The Eurodollar System* (London: Macmillan, 1973).

10. E. W. Clendenning, *The Euro-Dollar Market* (Oxford University Press, 1970).

11. R. F. Mikesell and J. H. Furth, *Foreign Dollar Balances and the International Role of the Dollar* (New York: National Bureau of Economic Research, 1974).

12. B. S. Quinn, *The New Euro Markets* (London: Macmillan, 1975).

CHAPTER TWO

1. 'Eurodollars – an Important Source of Funds For American Banks', *Federal Reserve Bank of Chicago Monthly Review* (June 1969).

2. For criticism of this tendency, cf. F. Machlup, 'Euro-dollar creation: A Mystery Story', *Banca Nazionale del Lavoro Quarterly Review* (Sep 1970) pp. 219–60.

3. P. Einzig, *The Eurodollar System* (London: Macmillan, 1973).

4. G. McKenzie, *The Monetary Theory of International Trade* (London: Macmillan, 1974).

5. I. F. Pearce, *International Trade* Bk. I, (London: Macmillan, 1970).

6. D. Hume, 'Of The Balance of Trade', *Essays, Moral, Political and*

Literary, vol. 1 (London: Longmans, Green, 1898) reprinted in *International Finance*, ed. R. N. Cooper (Harmondsworth: Penguin, 1969).

7. H. G. Johnson, 'The Monetary Approach to Balance of Payments Theory', in *International Trade and Money*, ed. M. Connolly and A. Swoboda (London: Allen & Unwin, 1973).

8. International Monetary Fund, *Balance of Payments Manual* (Washington, D.C., 1961).

9. Review Committee for Balance of Payments Statistics to the Bureau of the Budget, *The Balance of Payments Statistics of the United States* (Washington, D.C., U.S. Government Printing Office, 1965).

CHAPTER THREE

1. I. F. Pearce, *International Trade* (London: Macmillan, 1970).

2. P. Davidson, *Money and the Real World* (London: Macmillan, 1972).

3. J. R. Hicks, 'Recollections and Documents', *Economica*, 40 (Feb 1973) pp. 2–11.

4. Karl Brunner and Allan Meltzer, 'The Uses of Money: Money in a Theory of an Exchange Economy', *American Economic Review*, 61 (Dec 1971) pp. 784–805.

5. William Silber, 'Innovations in the Financial Sector', Working Paper No. 31, Salomon Brothers Center for the Study of Financial Institutions (Mar 1975).

6. Irving Fisher, *The Theory of Interest* (New York: Macmillan, 1930).

7. Joseph Conard, *An Introduction to the Theory of Interest* (University of California Press, 1966).

CHAPTER FOUR

1. Arthur Burns, 'Statement before the U.S. Senate Committee on Banking, Housing and Urban Affairs', reprinted in the *Federal Reserve Bulletin* (Mar 1975).

2. Hyman Minsky, 'Financial Crisis, Financial Systems, and the Performance of the Economy', in *Private Capital Markets*, Commission on Money and Credit (Englewood Cliffs, N.J.: Prentice-Hall, 1964).

3. P. Davidson, *Money and the Real World* (London: Macmillan, 1972).

4. M. Friedman and A. J. Schwartz, *A Monetary History of the United States, 1867–1960* (Princeton University Press, 1963) especially pp. 351 ff.

5. A. K. Swoboda, *The Euro-dollar Market: An Interpretation*, Essays in International Finance, no. 64 (Princeton University, Feb 1968) and 'Vehicle Currencies and the Foreign Exchange Market: The Case of the Dollar', in *The International Market for Foreign Exchange*, ed. Robert E. Aliber (New York: Praeger, 1969).

6. Swoboda, 'Vehicle Currencies and the Foreign Exchange Market: The Case of the Dollar'.

CHAPTER FIVE

1. 'A New Measure of the Money Stock', *Federal Reserve Bulletin* (Oct 1960) pp. 1102–13, this quotation p. 1103.
2. 'Revision of Money Supply Series', *Federal Reserve Bulletin* (Aug 1962) pp. 941–5, this quotation p. 944.
3. A. E. Burger and Anatol Balbach, 'Measure of the Domestic Money Stock', *Review of the Federal Reserve Bank of St Louis* (May 1972) pp. 10–23.
4. A. A. Alchian and W. Allen, *University Economics* (Belmont, California: Wadsworth, 1968).
5. H. G. Johnson, 'The Monetary Approach to Balance of Payments Theory', in *International Trade and Money*, ed. M. Connolly and A. Swoboda (London: Allen & Unwin, 1973).

CHAPTER SIX

1. J. Tobin, 'Commercial Banks as Creators of "Money" ', in *Banking and Monetary Studies*, ed. D. Carson (Homewood, Ill.: Irwin, 1963) pp. 408–19.
2. A. K. Swoboda, *The Euro-Dollar Market: An Interpretation*, Essays in International Finance, no. 64 (Princeton University, Feb 1968).
3. Milton Friedman, 'The Euro-Dollar Market: Some First Principles', *Morgan Guaranty Survey* (Oct 1969) pp. 4–14; reprinted in the *Review of the Federal Reserve Bank of St Louis*, 53 (July 1971) pp. 16–24.
4. H. Mayer, 'Multiplier Effects and Credit Creation in the Euro-Dollar Market', *Banca Nazionale del Lavoro Quarterly Review* (Sep 1971) pp. 233–62.
5. E. W. Clendenning, 'Euro-Dollars and Credit Creation', *International Currency Review*, 3 (Mar–Apr 1971) pp. 12–19.
6. J. Hewson and E. Sakakibara, 'The Euro-Dollar Deposit Multiplier: A Portfolio Approach', *Internetional Monetary Fund Staff Papers*, 22 (March 1975) pp. 37–60.
7. Tobin, 'Commercial Banks as Creators of "Money" '.
8. Friedman, 'The Euro-Dollar Market: Some First Principles'.
9. F. H. Klopstock, *The Euro-Dollar Market: Some Unresolved Issues*, Essays in International Finance, no. 65 (Princeton University, Mar 1968).
10. F. H. Klopstock, 'Money Creation in the Euro-Dollar Market – A Note on Professor Friedman's Views', *Review of the Federal Reserve Bank of New York*, 52 (Jan 1970) pp. 12–15.
11. Mayer, 'Multiplier Effects and Credit Creation in the Euro-Dollar Market', pp. 236–7.
12. Swoboda, *The Euro-Dollar Market: An Interpretation*.
13. Mayer, 'Multiplier Effects and Credit Creation in the Euro-Dollar Market', p. 237.
14. Clendenning, 'Euro-Dollars and Credit Creation'.
15. Hewson and Sakakibara, 'The Euro-Dollar Deposit Multiplier: A Portfolio Approach'.

16. Mayer, 'Multiplier Effects and Credit Creation in the Euro-Dollar Market', p. 236.

17. Klopstock, *The Euro-Dollar Market: Some Unresolved Issues*, p. 8.

18. Hewson and Sakakibara, 'The Euro-Dollar Deposit Multiplier: A Portfolio Approach'.

CHAPTER SEVEN

1. W. Silber, 'Innovations in the Financial Sector', Working Paper No. 31, Salomon Brothers Center for the Study of Financial Institutions (Mar 1975).

2. P. Einzig, *History of Foreign Exchange* (London: Macmillan, 1962).

3. O. L. Altman, 'Recent Developments in Foreign Markets for Dollars and Other Currencies', in *Factors Affecting the United States Balance of Payments*, Joint Economic Committee of the 87th U.S. Congress (Washington: U.S. Government Printing Office, 1962) pp. 485–523.

4. A. Swoboda, 'Vehicle Currencies and the Foreign Exchange Market: The Case of the Dollar', in *The International Market for Foreign Exchange*, ed. Robert E. Aliber (New York: Praeger, 1969).

5. O. L. Altman, 'Foreign Markets for Dollars, Sterling and Other Currencies', *International Monetary Fund Staff Papers*, 8 (Dec 1961) pp. 313–52; 'Recent Developments in Foreign Markets for Dollars, Sterling and Other Currencies', *International Monetary Fund Staff Papers*, 10 (Mar 1963) pp. 48–96; and 'Euro-Dollars – Some Further Comments', *International Monetary Fund Staff Papers*, 12 (Mar 1965) pp. 1–16.

6. H. H. Schloss, 'The Bank for International Settlements', *Bulletin of the Schools of Business of New York University*, nos 65–6 (Sep 1970).

7. P. Einzig, *The Eurodollar System* (London: Macmillan, 1973).

8. Bank for International Settlements, *Thirty-Fourth Annual Report* (Basle, 1964) p. 132.

9. M. Friedman, 'The Euro-Dollar Market: Some First Principles', *Morgan Guaranty Survey* (Oct 1969) pp. 4–14; reprinted in *Review of the Federal Reserve Bank of St Louis*, 53 (July 1971) pp. 16–24, this quotation p. 16.

10. F. H. Klopstock, 'Money Creation in the Euro-Dollar Market – A Note on Professor Friedman's Views', *Review of the Federal Reserve Bank of New York* (Jan 1970) pp. 12–15, this quotation p. 14.

11. C. P. Kindleberger, *International Economics*, 5th edn (Homewood, Ill.: Irwin, 1973).

12. C. A. Coombs, 'Treasury and Federal Reserve Foreign Exchange Operations', *Review of the Federal Reserve Bank of New York* (Mar 1968) pp. 38–52, this quotation p. 50.

13. J. Heinz *et al.*, 'Recent Innovations in European Capital Markets', *Review of the Federal Reserve Bank of New York* (Jan 1965) pp. 9–15, this quotation p. 10.

CHAPTER EIGHT

1. M. Willms, 'Controlling Money in an Open Economy: The German Case', *Review of the Federal Reserve Bank of St Louis* (Apr 1971) pp. 10–27.

2. R. Mundell, *International Economics* (New York: Macmillan, 1968).

3. J. H. Furth, 'International Monetary Reform and the "Crawling Peg": Comment', *Review of the Federal Reserve Bank of St Louis* (July 1969) pp. 21–5, this quotation p. 22.

4. W. Branson, 'The Minimum Covered Interest Differential Needed for International Arbitrage Activity', *Journal of Political Economy* (Nov–Dec 1969) pp. 1028–35.

5. Willms, 'Controlling Money in an Open Economy: The German Case'.

6. H. Schlesinger and H. Bockelmann, 'Monetary Policy in the Federal Republic of Germany', in *Monetary Policy in Twelve Industrial Countries*, ed. K. Holbik (Federal Reserve Bank of Boston, 1973).

7. R. M. Mills, 'The Regulation of Short-Term Capital Movements: Western European Techniques in the 1960's', *Staff Economic Studies*, no. 46, Board of Governors of the Federal Reserve System, Washington, D.C. (1968).

8. Organization for Economic Co-operation and Development, 'Controls on Capital Flows', *Economic Outlook* (Dec 1972) pp. 71–7.

9. S. I. Katz, ' "Managed Floating" As an Interim International Exchange Rate Regime, 1973–1975', *Bulletin of the Schools of Business of New York University*, no. 3 (1975).

10. M. Friedman, 'The Case for Flexible Exchange Rates', in his *Essays in Positive Economics* (Chicago University Press, 1953) pp. 157–203.

11. The source for Figure 8.2 is the Bank for International Settlements, *Annual Report* (1974–5) p. 11.

12. Bank for International Settlements, *Annual Report* (1974–5).

CHAPTER NINE

1. R. N. Cooper, *The Economics of Interdependence* (New York: McGraw-Hill, 1968).

2. J. C. Ingram, 'A Proposal for Financial Integration in the Atlantic Community', in *Factors Affecting the United States Balance of Payments*, Joint Economic Committee of the Congress of the United States (Washington D.C., 1962).

Index